CW00544256

Home to Rome

A short account of a long walk

HOME TO
ROME
MAP

Matador
Unit E2 Airfield Business Park,
Harrison Road, Market Harborough,
Leicestershire. LE16 7WB
Tel: 01162 792299
Email: books@troubador.co.uk
Web: www.troubador.co.uk/matador
Twitter: @matadorbooks

ISBN 978 1803130 477

British Library Cataloguing in Publication Data.
A catalogue record for this book is available from the British Library.

Printed and bound by CPI Group (UK) Ltd, Croydon, CR0 4YY

Matador is an imprint of Troubador Publishing Ltd

For The Keeper
And all our friends who joined us on the walk

Why Walk from Home to Rome?

“Is there anything in particular you want to do next summer?” asked my husband of twenty-eight years. I sat back in the armchair and thought about his question. What would I really like to do, or more importantly, what would we both really like to do?

“Give me a minute and I'll think about it,” I said as I left the room to make a cup of tea. Returning with two cups of builders, I also returned with the answer.

“I would like to walk to Rome. With you.”

He spilt his tea. And then looked at me with such wide-eyed delight I thought for a minute I had accidently offered something other than a long walk.

“Where from?” he asked, trying hard to suppress the edge of excitement in his voice, containing any further enthusiasm until the full facts and parameters of my suggestion were established.

“From here, from home. Why don't we just walk out of the door and keep going until we arrive in Rome?”

Long walks were not new to us. Five years prior, on the American Appalachian Trail, we had not only picked up fleas but a chronic desire for a second adolescence on foot.

We had trodden many a road since then, but our adolescent symptoms, which included the need to stride and the desire to perspire outdoors, were a long way from being cured.

“Hmmm,” he replied, mulling it over, his mathematical brain already at work calculating likely routes and distances and plotting them against time needed. “Why Rome and why from here?”

I sat back down in the armchair. The answer was easy: tea, wine and architecture. Our two previous long-distance hikes had been remote. For days on end, we had not seen another soul, let alone the red nectar found inside a wine bottle. I wanted to wake to tea, to walk through historical splendour and to sleep each night in a bed, having sampled (in small amounts, obviously) the 'divine liquor of the grape', as Leonardo Da Vinci put it. In short, this time I wanted a civilised walk.

Oh, and I also wanted that delicious feeling of freedom right from the word go. Freedom from planes, trains and automobiles. We would simply close the front door of our home in Hampshire and walk all the way to Rome.

"So, you are serious then?" he asked.

"Yes, I'm serious," I replied.

That was all that was needed. A that-is-exciting grin, freed from its containment of uncertainty, swept across my husband's face. We had decided to walk to Rome, to have a summer of hard physical activity, to shed (for a short time anyway) the trappings of a life of multiplicity and to stride forth in simplicity.

The door banged as he left the room to research how exactly one walks to Rome. I stayed and finished my tea.

Trail Names: Mountain Goat and The Keeper

A long-distance trail is a great leveller. It is just you and your backpack with an absence of the usual indicators of position or wealth: you are not lugging a house, a car or a career. You meet fellow hikers in the rain and discuss good shelter points; you meet in the heat of the day and you share water. You are judged on your actions and your ability to add levity to life. No one really cares who you are off the trail so why ask your real name on the trail? Given names that comment on your actions are far more informative.

We have met some wonderful characters: Stop for Berries, Sunny Day and Patches. How do you get these names? They find you.

I was hiking a mountain in Maine, USA, attempting to get down a steep wall of scree, when my trail name found me. Other, younger hikers were effortlessly springing their way down, jumping gazelle-like across the scree. I looked at them and decided that their method was not for me. I went down the only way I knew how; bottom first. And the scree came with me. At the bottom, as I lay in a heap of triumph and stones, I felt for sure that I was equal in stature to the young around me. Then a passing gazelle asked, with concern, if I was alright. Bending over and offering me his hand, he pulled me to my feet, commenting that I had done well getting down. Which is where he should have left things but with youthful exuberance, he added, "As you are clearly no mountain goat."

Mountain Goat stuck and I left my christened name and my ego behind me on that mountain.

A draconian desire to have sole charge of all the maps, to adhere to the timetable and crush the enemy of spontaneity left someone else open to a bit of ribbing. The title of 'The Keeper of the Maps' or 'The Keeper' for short, swiftly found its way to my other half.

And so there it is, as easily as picking up a dose of scabies, we had picked up our trail names: Mountain Goat and The Keeper.

Planning the Route

The kitchen table became the general headquarters for the advance on Rome. From there, guidebooks were ordered, blogs were read and maps unfolded to their full glory. So many maps that, to regain some table territory, we had to cut them down to the linear strips of what was to be our world. In a car, you might want to know about an appealing diversion 10km away; on foot, you need to know only what lies directly in front of you.

With the how in hand, we explored the 'if and when'. Gathering our three children and their partners around us, we shared our plans. As The Keeper excitedly talked, I watched the familial faces in front of us. An arched eyebrow went up and down the line, followed by a candid look of amusement between the siblings. I read their unspoken words. *The olds are off again, but if it floats their boat....* Sure enough, they hugged their approval.

We then considered all the other aspects of what makes up a 21st century life and began juggling. Work commitments, social commitments (when exactly was The Keeper's niece getting married?) and who was going to look after the dog? Paying homage to the weather as well, an eighty day window crystalised in our diaries.

We were going to leave our home on 1 July, 2018 (at 08:00 according to The Keeper of all things time-related) and arrive in Rome on 15 September (at noon, apparently), seventy-seven straight days of walking and no rest days. We would be following the North Downs Way to Canterbury and the Via Francigena from Canterbury to Rome.

But hang on, the guidebooks recommended ninety days for just Canterbury to Rome. Were we really going to add on the home to Canterbury bit and still do it two weeks faster? We revisited the published miles; we restudied the published maps. If the guidebook data were true, we thought we could do it. We sealed the deal with a cup of tea and a shared moment of anxiety hastily pushed away with a chocolate digestive.

Data collection, exploration and manipulation is one of The Keeper's key skills and he put it to good use. A spreadsheet magnus opus was created, which I was invited to admire but not touch. Each day's destination, mileage and lodging were recorded with my request for an average 17 miles per day noted and heeded. It is a shame the reality differed, but that is for later.

And there, in black and white, was my ultimate wish. We had lodgings. I was not going to have to carry a tent, or a stove or even a bedroll. I could bathe; I could sleep between sheets; I could be civilised.

But why limit this incredible (as we saw it) journey to just us? Our enthusiasm led us to send the following email to all our walking comrades-in-boots.

Mountain Goat and I will be setting off on a walk through England, France, Switzerland and Italy. Our previous long walks have been largely solitary affairs, but we are hoping to have friends and family join us for parts of Home to Rome.

Very broadly, the plan is as follows:
1 July: set off early on local paths to Farnham
2 July: start the North Downs Way to Canterbury
8 July: arrive in Canterbury and drink beer
9 July: reach Dover, catch ferry to Calais
20 July: arrive in Reims and drink Champagne
5 August: cross Jura Mountains, into Switzerland and eat chocolate
7 August: arrive in Lausanne
12 August: climb Col du Grand St Bernard, and into Italy for a pasta extravaganza
17 August: start the Piedmont region, sampling the wines, cheeses, truffles...
27 August: over the Passo della Cisa and into Tuscany
8 September: reach Siena, continuing to enjoy Italian cuisine, wine and culture
16 September: arrive in Rome, and dispose of walking boots

Thirty-seven of our intrepid friends booked onto 'The Gourmet's Guide to Hiking' and joined for various stages along the way. Some of them even did some training.

ENGLISH CHANNEL
HOME
Canterbury
Dover
Calais
Thérouanne
Arras
Péronne
Laon
Reims
Châlons-en-Champagne
Brienne-le-Château
Bar-Sur-Aube
Langres
Champlitte
Besançon
Lausanne
Montreux
Col du Grand-Saint-Bernard
Aosta
Ivrea
Pavia
Piacenza
Fidenza
Fornovo di Taro
Berceto
Pontremoli
Lucca
San Gimignano
Siena
Bolsena
ROMA
ADRIATIC SEA
BAY OF BISCAY
TYRRHENIAN SEA
N
E
S
W

The Footpaths

The North Downs Way

The North Downs Way runs from Farnham in Hampshire to Dover in Kent and is one of the fifteen National Trails or Long-Distance Routes of England and Wales. The first of these long-distance trails was the Pennine Way, opened in 1965, and the most recent is the England Coast Path, which is still under construction.

The Pilgrims Way

The Pilgrims Way is the historical route taken by pilgrims from Winchester in Hampshire to the shrine of Thomas Becket at Canterbury in Kent.

The Via Francigena

The Via Francigena is an ancient route, a virtual straight line running in a south-easterly direction between Canterbury and Rome. It crosses half a continent and four countries: England, France, Switzerland and Italy. From Canterbury, it travels over the Kent Downs to Dover and then across the English Channel to Calais and northern France. It winds through the WWI battlefields of Picardy and then through the Champagne region before entering Switzerland over the Juras. Skirting Lac Léman to approach the Alps, it crosses the Grand St Bernard Pass, descending into Italy down the Aosta Valley to Piedmont and Lombardy, and finally over the Apennines and the hills of Tuscany to end in Rome.

As a pilgrimage route, it is described as the hardcore version of the Camino de Santiago in Spain and, as such, is far less travelled.

At the end of the 10th century, Sigeric the Serious, Archbishop of Canterbury, needed to fetch his pallium from the Pope. As FedEx was unavailable, he went himself and used the Via Francigena to travel to Rome. On his return, he recorded his journey and the places where he stopped in a document which is now in the British Museum. His itinerary lists the eighty place names he visited, and this defines the route of the Via Francigena of today.

The Pilgrim's Passport

The credential or pilgrim's passport is the identity card of the modern-day pilgrim. It is not a legal document but more of a certification of 'pilgrim' status. We chose to pre-arrange and book our lodgings before we started our journey. However, many pilgrims rely on the hosting generosity at refuges and monastic buildings for their accommodation. By getting the passport stamped every night at tourist offices, churches or hostels, the pilgrim builds up authentic proof of the journey undertaken thus far. Arriving at the door of accommodating facilities with a pilgrim's passport gains you access and often supper.

The pilgrim's identification document is not a new-fangled commercial gimmick. The credentials once existed as badges made from pewter or tin. They were worn as a sign of devotion and as proof of the accomplished journey.

We carried our pilgrim passports and had them stamped every night. This proof of our long journey would be needed to gain access to the final stamp, that of the Vatican's. We were not expecting a pallium ourselves but thought a T-shirt might come in handy.

The Kit

We were going to have to carry everything, yes everything, we needed for seventy-seven days. From experience, we knew the advantages of travelling light. Our first challenge, therefore, was going to be just how light could we go? We started putting everything we thought we needed onto a spare bed.

"Do you really need this?" I asked The Keeper, holding up his netted anti-mosquito hat.

"It's only light," he responded, but I noticed he surreptitiously took it off the bed.

"Do you need this? Is it really essential?" The Keeper asked, holding up my hair volumising mousse. I pondered the question. Sitting on my bathroom shelf at home, the mousse would come under the classification of essential. Lugging it on my back for hundreds of miles? Forget it, The Keeper was right, and I slipped it off the bed (when he was not looking). I also removed the soap, shampoo and conditioner, hoping we would get these where we stayed, leaving limited toiletries and basic medicines. I added a comb (for me) as a brush was too heavy, and The Keeper's unique hairstyle required neither.

Two packs for each of us landed on the bed, one for the back and a smaller waist pack for the front. We like front packs as they are handy for those things needed more often such as our phones, sunglasses, snacks, tissues, water bottles (all of which also got put on the bed).

Then even more items were added: maps, guidebook, compass, phone charger, sun hat and a waterproof document wallet. With the Alps in mind, we added a rain jacket, lightweight skull cap, lightweight gloves, a whistle and foil blanket.

After slight uncertainty from The Keeper but certainty from me, we decided to carry walking poles. I prefer being a four-legged animal rather than a two-legged one. To a Mountain Goat it feels more stable.

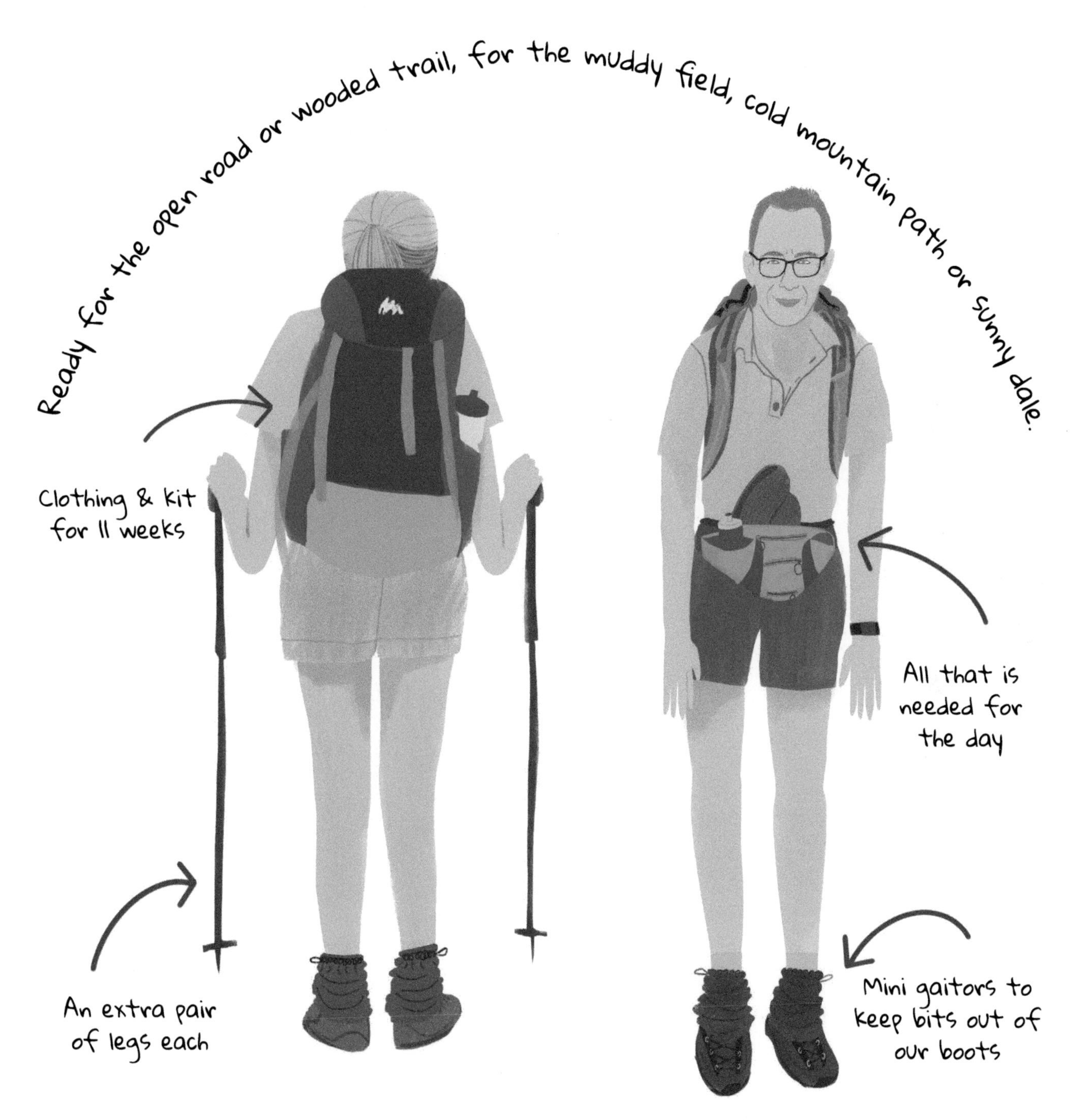
Ready for the open road or wooded trail, for the muddy field, cold mountain path or sunny dale.
Clothing & kit for 11 weeks
All that is needed for the day
An extra pair of legs each
Mini gaitors to keep bits out of our boots

With the space on the bed getting smaller, we turned to our clothes: what was truly essential in the wardrobe department? Underwear, of course, is essential to me, but I am not so sure about The Keeper. But how many pieces? We would be hand-washing each night, so with some pontification I chose just two pairs, one on and one in the pack. The Keeper chose the first two that happened to be sitting on the top of his drawer.

For our other clothes, the same idea followed: walking tops - one on, one in the bag. Socks? Yep, one pair on, one in the bag. Some items did not justify being doubled up. Walking shorts and a lightweight fleece came singly. We also needed something to wear in the evenings. What could we get away with? We decided on lightweight soft shoes (that we could also walk in if our boots gave out), a dress for me, shorts and a shirt for The Keeper. I trawled the internet for the lightest items I could find, rejecting weight-bearing sleeves, belts, zips and sex appeal.

A shapeless shift dress and flat, strapped sandals arrived at our door, thrown from a passing cement mixer, by the look of them. I tried the dress on in front of the mirror and instantly wished I had not. A lentil-eating earth mother, fresh from a composting toilet, had joined in the fun. I snuck in the luxury of a hair-tie and a lip gloss; not sufficient, I know, to transform composter to supermodel, but desperation is the mother of imagination.

Finally, with everything assembled on the bed, we began to pack. I separated my items into several lightweight waterproof bags so that everything was ordered and organised. The Keeper opened his backpack and tipped everything in.

hand cream
LIP GLOSS
BODY LOTION
500ml
Hair Mousse

DAY 1

Date: Sunday 1 July

Start: 07:30 at Home

Finish: 16:00 at Crondall

Distance: 35.8km (22.4 miles)

Total: 36km (22 miles)

Daily average: 35.8km (22.4 miles)

Day one had arrived. I woke early with a knot in my stomach and a head full of things to do. Had I treated the dog for fleas, cleaned out the fridge, left enough bin liners for the house sitters?

With my lamentable earth mother outfit packed in my backpack, I put on my only other set of clothes for the next two and a half months: a beige shirt, khaki shorts, walking socks, boots and a hat... Livingstone's aunty. Just then, The Keeper walked in dressed and ready, the uncle to my aunt. We were prepared for the Nile as well as the good paths of Hampshire.

The Keeper prescribes to the 'less choice, more freedom' philosophy when it comes to wardrobe management. The less he has, the more time is saved from choosing what to wear, ergo more time to do other things. He was whistling with joy in the knowledge that he only had two shirts (one for the day and one for the evening) to rotate from now to Rome.

I, on the other hand, have a different approach to wardrobe management. Its upkeep and restocking are activities I enjoy. I like to dress up for dinner or down for the weekend, to occasionally put on a pretty outfit and feel feminine.

Not from today though; for the next two and a half months, my wardrobe would be a mere memory - I was to be aunty by day and earth mother by night. I took a minute to say farewell to my soft shoes and silky tops, my handbags and jewellery, then I hoisted up my backpack and went downstairs.

Mid-muesli, knowing The Keeper's attachment to promptness, our friends and neighbours started arriving to see us off. Soon the morning was punctuated with wishes of good luck and requests for cups of coffee. At 07:55, taking a subtle hint from The Keeper, who was walking around 'Nile ready', we all moved to the porch. With a cheer from those intrepid friends who were joining us for the day, and those just there for the coffee, we closed the front door and stepped off the porch. That first step was the first of our adventure, the first of what would eventually be 1.8 million steps to Rome.

Whilst others around me set off full of the chatter that comes with the promise of only a day's outing, I was quieter. We were leaving for seventy-seven days. I mentally ticked off all those jobs I thought I had to do. A final minute of jurisdiction over my home before leaving it to the care of others. Had I checked the house sitters for fleas, put the dog in the fridge and cleaned the bin liners? Probably not, but there was little I could do now.

We had inadvertently chosen one of the hottest British summers on record and the temperature was already rising. With The Keeper out front, assuming the position that validated his name (and which we were all secretly grateful for as it meant, like Lemmings, we only had to follow and not think), we set off to find Basingstoke and its canal. Our route took us across fields and through villages that were lying in a haze of abandonment, their inhabitants having already given in to the heat and sought refuge in shade or armchairs.

We were joined by other friends along the way so that, by lunchtime, there were fifteen of us sitting at a pub table, diving into piles of sandwiches and chips.

The remaining afternoon hours were spent in a happy state of walking, more chatting and ice-cream sampling, until arriving at our destination, the village of Crondall.

Over the years we have found that as a group, walkers or hikers are often misunderstood fellows who are frequently miscategorised under the heading of 'waif and stray'. We are seen as anorak-wearing do-gooders whose only conversation is the various merits of Gore-Tex and the state of our secondary glazing. We were reminded of this phenomenon on that first night.

Our original B&B, getting a hint of the idea that we might be walkers and therefore social misfits, or even, heaven forbid, poor (just why were they carless?), cancelled on us at the last minute. We were sent on our way to another B&B. At the door of this substitute, the customary welcome was left under the hallway carpet, and we were greeted with, "We are only doing this as a favour, you know." We were then shown around the side of the house and into the garden. As we crossed the terrace, our host pointed out a charming barn conversion at the end of the lawn; it was picture perfect, an idyll of rambling roses, soft hewn wood and cane sun loungers.

"That's where we usually put our paying guests but not you. You're in the attic of the house, which is up those stairs."

Travelling on foot sometimes reduces the extent to which you can be forthright. We needed that room, so we held our tongues, smiled and went to find 'those stairs'.

We were shown through the back of the house and to the laundry room that was piled high with clothes waiting to be processed. We threaded our way through the dirty items trying not to smell the socks or hook our poles on the 'smalls' and made our way up the stairs to our bedroom. The bedroom, we discovered, was not only above the kitchen but also directly above the furnace of their Aga. Of course, what well-respected English family turns their Aga off, even in 30+ degrees!

We opened both undersized windows that came with the room and prayed for a breeze or even the offer of a cold drink. What we got was a knock at the door and a "That will be cash only, please."

DAY 2

Date: Monday 2 July

Start: 05:30 at Crondall

Finish: 15:00 at Newlands Corner

Distance: 33.7km (21.6 miles)

Total: 70km (43 miles)

Daily average: 34.7km (21.7 miles)

Thanks to the unwanted sauna, we had spent the night turning in perspiration like two oversized hens on a rotisserie. We left our room with relief, short on rest and a kilo lighter than when we had entered. Enjoying the fresh morning air, we walked into Crondall and met up with Jane (affectionately known by the trail name of 'Chumley'), a long-term friend and walker extraordinaire. By the time most people were contemplating their cornflakes, we had covered the 5 miles into Farnham, had a coffee and found the start of the North Downs Way. A busy junction of the A31 is an unusual choice for the start of a National Trail but the good councillors of Farnham must have had their reasons. Perhaps, in retribution, or to entice car drivers, they had installed a splendid celebratory structure. Five free-standing Corten steel sheets had been erected, announcing the North Downs Way and showing an arrow to the finish, Dover, 153 miles away. Feeling that we had reached a milestone, I weaved with glee in and out of the weathered steel as Chumley, The Keeper and passing locals looked on.

We picked up the path, reflecting on a comment we had overheard earlier in the coffee shop: "Look at their backpacks. It says Home to Rome. They can't be walking to Rome; it must be a typo." Well, we were truly on our way now and living that typo.

The North Downs, that we were now following, is a ridge of chalk hills that stretches from Hampshire through Surrey to Kent. In parts now protected, they are beautiful and ancient, a downland covered in species-rich turf containing equally ancient supermarkets and pharmacies. There are edible plants like marjoram, wild thyme, and salad burnet. And medicinal plants like eyebright and the delightfully named squinancywort or sore throat plant.

However, today was mostly suburbia: leafy roads of large houses, paths besides golf courses and tracks through broken woodland.

Chumley left us at Guildford, and we trundled on to St Martha's Church upon the hill, where we were met by The Keeper's brother, Mark. St Martha's is a spectacularly positioned church set alone on one of the highest points on the Downs. It had been a bit of a climb to get there, for Mark as well; St Martha's does not see the need for vehicular access, relying on all its visitors to approach on foot. We knew Mark would be there however, as he had done the climb before in September 1981, his wedding day. His bride in full trail and veil, you will be pleased to know, had forsaken her feet, sought dispensation and arrived squashed into a 4x4.

We stood together, our backs to the church, enjoying its view, an open vista across rolling countryside of deep blue sky, parched grassland and low-flying pizza delivery boxes. Strapped to the back of an enterprising young man with a mountain bike, and hopefully a sense of direction, the passing margherita mirage surprised us all.

Our second night was spent in a hotel just off the North Downs Way. It was a great find if you were a Turkish salesman and pining for a bit of the motherland. Gold ceilings and shiny flock wallpaper were in abundance. It was not such a find if you were a vegetarian. Burgundy in colour, our thin bedding made us feel like we were slipping between layers of sliced liver to sleep.

DAY 3

Date: Tuesday 3 July

Start: 05:30 at Gomshall

Finish: 15:00 at Merstham

Distance: 34.5km (21.6 miles)

Total: 104km (65 miles)

Daily average: 34.7km (21.7 miles)

To beat the predicted but unprecedented heat of the day, we rose early from our offal bed and headed out. In the clarity that so often comes with the morning light, the open views across the downland were striking. You cannot quantify the joy that comes from a perfect view, it fills you with a happiness that is almost tangible. In this positive state we continued, the path very kindly mixing our morning between downland and the welcome shade of ancient woodland.

Then, as if to put the cherry on the cake of our day, we came across a vineyard. The vineyard entered our lives just as the need for a cup of tea (it was only 10:00) entered our heads. And, luckily, amongst its many offerings was a cafe. Thanking the trail gods, we headed off across the vineyard using the nearest access, which happened to be signed 'employees only'. The disadvantage of being on foot is that official entrances lying a good mile away are nonoptimal. The advantages of being on foot, middle-aged and wearing a backpack, is that you appear to others as quite benign. An image that, if called upon, you can work to your advantage in times of great need. Tea, we reasoned, is a great need.

Fortified with tea, we left the vineyard, passing by the wine bottles we could not fit in our backpacks. We were heading for Box Hill, a summit of the North Downs; the weight of a wine bottle was not something I needed just then, or ever. The hill gets its name from the ancient box woodland found on its steepest west-facing slope. We were halfway up this slope in our usual climbing formation (The Keeper upfront with me trailing behind) when I was joined by a charming young man from Singapore.

This adventurous man had landed at Gatwick, walked out of the airport, and just kept on walking. His plan was to reach Canterbury on foot before getting the train to London and catching up with friends. Although carrying a backpack, any further resemblance to each other as fellow hikers stopped there. He looked like he had just stepped out of a Ralph Lauren advert with sharply pressed chinos, a dazzlingly white polo shirt and every single hair on his head lying in controlled order. Perspiration, if he made any, was happening somewhere unseen.

He climbed beside me, chatting away politely as I puffed and panted my way up, a vision of sweat and disorder. Between my puffs, he gathered that I and the odd-looking chap up ahead were on our way to Rome. Concern filled his eyes. *Did we know how far this was?* I confirmed that we were not without some geographical knowledge and yes, we knew how far it was. With extreme politeness, he gently asked my age. Hearing my answer, he stopped suddenly and announced, "But that is as old as my father and even older than my mother! They would not attempt such a thing." Implying, I think, that at our age, we should not be attempting it either.

Then, without another word, he sprinted off into the distance and was never seen again. I pondered this prompt departure. Was it because he feared the risk of having to deal with a cardiac arrest on a British hillside? Or was it because he believed adventures were only the prerogative of the young? We will never know, but I hope his view of his parents' ambitions and capabilities has been challenged.

DAY 4

Date: Wednesday 4 July

Start: 07:30 at Merstham

Finish: 15:30 at Otford

Distance: 32.4km (20.3 miles)

Total: 136km (85 miles)

Daily average: 34.1km (21.3 miles)

I woke up still tingling with yesterday's positivity; we had got this far, we were still fit, still happy with our plans and still talking to each other. A cause for celebration, served up with a piece of haddock for breakfast.

On the road, we passed over Merstham Station looking down at the platform from a bridge. I could see the commuters, a latte in one hand and an air of resignation in the other. But what I really noticed were their shoes, they all wore them. Nice, soft, clean shoes that looked very appealing. My feet were encased in big, brown, earth-caked clodhoppers. I thought about footwear and its implications. Did I want to stop right there and swap my vulcanised, rubber soled boots for smooth, red leather soled shoes? It was tempting but I realised the answer was no. I had made my choice: I was going to wear clodhoppers for the next seventy plus days and I was content, in fact I was happy. The hardwiring of modern life, the deadlines, bills, technology and consumption, even the need to wear shoes, I realised, was beginning to unravel with each new day on the road.

The positivity stayed with me even though it was not the favourite of our days so far. It was hard going and shared with the M25, M23, A22 and M26. We walked through the vestiges of countryside trapped within these motorway systems and saw glimpses of outstanding beauty. However, the constant drone of traffic and the views interrupted by trails of cars took the edge off the pleasure of the hike.

I was ready for the sight of our hotel when it came into view, even if it did have a bad case of schizophrenia. Two large stone Indian elephants and neon lighting in front of a pseudo-Tudor manor house were confusing but not off-putting. We went in and found a happy mix of English mock architecture and Indian bling; a sort of tomato ketchup meets mango chutney world which we made our own for the night.

DAY 5

Date: Thursday 5 July

Start: 05:30 at Otford

Finish: 13:00 at Cuxton

Distance: 29.3km (18.3 miles)

Total: 166km (104 miles)

Daily average: 33.1km (20.7 miles)

During our first four days of walking, a right of ownership had been firmly established over the spreadsheet and the maps: The Keeper had the rights; I did not. This natural (to him) state was put into question on our fifth day.

We had started the day by climbing up into the bucolic hills of Kent and were rewarded for our efforts with big views and scenic walking. A glorious start that would normally have kept us delighted for hours, our backpack stores supplying all our needs for the day. However, the exceptional heat meant we were needing to refill our water supply more frequently and the desire for a cold drink was always present.

All was harmonious and at one in our little world until I saw a sign for, and put in a request to walk through, Trottiscliffe. The delightfully named Trottiscliffe has three notable features: the Coldrum Stones (a Neolithic burial ground), the medieval Church of St Peter and St Paul and, importantly on a hot day, not one but two pubs. *Not bad for a wee village and perfect timing,* thought I.

With thinly disguised patience, The Keeper of the Maps explained that we could not walk through that village, as it was on the Pilgrims Way, and we were following the North Downs Way (and hadn't I noticed this on the previous four days?).

With less thinly disguised patience, I pointed out that the Pilgrims Way ran alongside the North Downs Way and therefore would not be out of our way. We walked on, along the North Downs Way, The Keeper determinedly out front with me disgruntledly trundling behind as 'follower of The Keeper of the Maps' and 'Keeper of the Peace'.

We had been descending gently when, a little while later, we came to a crossroads, another sign and another choice in footpaths. There was the North Downs Way heading once more up into the hills, well out of the way of pesky villages and pubs serving ice-cold drinks. Or there was the Pilgrims Way which followed the lower contours of the land and did not miss a single hostelry or village shop (smart people, those pilgrims).

After a short and succinct discussion, with the added percussion of a little foot-stamping from me, we (just about) jointly agreed to follow the Pilgrims Way. I also established part ownership of the directions by downloading the OS maps onto my phone.

In the afternoon we reached the Medway and the town of Cuxton on its left bank. By then I was hotter than a bucket of jalapeños, with a thirst that the tepid water in my bottle could not abate. We staggered into the first pub we found, dropped our backpacks to the floor and drank, copiously. My pint of lime and soda did not stay long enough in the glass to make it worthwhile putting it there in the first place. The landlady should just have aimed the soda hose at my open mouth and taken it from there.

"I guess you were thirsty then," was the deadpan opening gambit from the landlady. Our polite nodding of the affirmative was enough to prompt a follow-up question. She raised an eyebrow and asked languidly, "Where are you going then?"

"To Rome," caused the other eyebrow to rise swiftly to the level of its partner.

We had the following conversation.

Landlady: "Really? Anything in particular you want to do in Rome?"

Us: "Not really."

Landlady: "How long are you going to stay when you get there?"

Us: "A weekend."

Landlady: "How long is it going to take you to get there?"

Us: "Seventy-seven days."

Landlady: "Did you think about flying?"

I could have shared the thought that sometimes a road is made for the journey and not the destination, but I thought it was perhaps best left for another day and ordered a further round of drinks instead.

Did you think about flying?

DAY 6

Date: Friday 6 July

Start: 07:30 at Cuxton

Finish: 14:30 at Bearsted

Distance: 24.5km (15.3 miles)

Total: 190km (119 miles)

Daily average: 31.7km (19.8 miles)

The morning's footpath played hide-and-seek with the transport system of the south-east until it could not hide any longer. Walking alongside the tarmac that links London with the Channel Tunnel, we came to a motorway junction and a backpack the size of a small caravan. Sitting in its shadow and smiling broadly at us was our friend 'Triathlete Pete'. Ex-military adventurist Pete had come prepared for all eventualities.

Together we crossed the Medway and headed down leafy tunnels away from the tarmac towards the country. It was not remarkable walking but it was made all the better by Pete's company, who was joining us for the next two days.

By a hot mid-morning, we had arrived in the village of Thurnham and at the door of the 14th Century Cock Inn. Unable to focus on anything other than a cold drink, we walked straight to the bar.

A 'how do' greeting, accompanied by a nod, came from two locals who were also at the bar. Dressed in tweed jackets and caps, the country camouflage of practicality that ignores weather and fashion idiosyncrasies, they looked us up and down.

"Out for a stroll then?" the larger of them asked.

"Yes, you could say that," I replied, more eager at that moment to down something cold than explain our stroll. With drinks in hand, we smiled and nodded politely and headed off to our seats.

I would not like to comment on the age of the two gentlemen, but I would take a guess that it had been some time since they and their teeth had slept together. It may also have been some time since their hearing had been checked, with their private conversation being less private than they imagined.

From across the pub, we could hear it all. "Did you see their packs? It says they are walking to Rome," said the smaller gentleman.

"Well, they are not doing that, you daft ha'porth. No one walks to Rome. You need your eyes testing you do." Admonished the larger gentleman.

Our thirst quenched, Pete and The Keeper headed for the door, but I delayed slightly and caught the eye of the smaller gentleman. Pointing to my Home to Rome badge, I gave him the thumbs up and nodded in the affirmative. He smiled delightedly. People do walk to Rome and, more importantly, he did not need his eyes tested.

From the inn, we continued to follow the historic Pilgrims Way. After the murder of Thomas Becket in Canterbury Cathedral in 1170, thousands of pilgrims followed the Pilgrims Way to St Thomas's shrine. Taverns and resting houses along the way were, effectively, the package holiday of the time.

Pete, assuming the role of captain to his newly found company, and despite the caravan on his back, set a military pace for the rest of the day. Before we knew it, we were in the pleasing village of Bearsted and, thankfully, at our modern version of a resting house for the night.

DAY 7

Date: Saturday 7 July

Start: 05:30 at Bearsted

Finish: 13:30 at Wye

Distance: 32.0km (20.0 miles)

Total: 222km (139 miles)

Daily average: 31.7km (19.8 miles)

A 05:30 departure meant I greeted the new day a little bleary-eyed and a tad footsore. Not so the chaps. Today was not only a FIFA World Cup day, but England were playing; an energy force of determination and anticipation emanated from their football-fuelled bodies.

Meticulous plans had been made the night before to ensure we would be in front of a television by the start of play. There was to be no deviation from these plans. My meek request for a quick cup of tea was met with such a withering response that I prudently went without.

We set off at a Pete pace and all was going well until a field of rapeseed swallowed our path.

The route across the field had not just been barred but obliterated by a farmer who obviously did not subscribe to *Hiking Monthly*.

As time was of the essence, and there was no apparent route around the field, we decided the only course of action was to cross it. We plunged in, each of us threading our own way through the triffid-like plants. The rapeseed was tall, the tops were the same height as my shoulders, and it was heavy with dried seed pods that scratched and lacerated my legs.

Getting to the other side of the field was a huge relief which I thought we might mark with a pause, a moment to catch our breath. Silly me, with no time for such nonsense, we picked up our path and marched on.

I did not leave the rapeseed trauma completely behind me, however. Within minutes my legs exploded into an itching red mass of criss-crossed welts. "Look at this," I cried, expecting sympathy but receiving none. The day's planning had not, apparently, made provision for allergic reactions and so my distress was ignored.

With only minutes to spare before kick-off the vision of Wye, our television destination, came into view. Instinctively, the chaps changed formation for maximum result. The Keeper of the Maps moved to the front, consulting and reconsulting the GPS, ensuring the most efficient route into the village. Triathlete Pete sat on his tail, adding his professional scouting skills (whenever he was allowed). Old elephant legs brought up the rear guard.

We found our pub and destination for the night, but it all looked surprisingly quiet. Dropping our rucksacks on the floor and racing to the bar, we asked, "What time are you starting the football?"

"We aren't," came the reply.

The idea of a pub not airing the game was so far-fetched that, like my legs, it had not been factored into the planning. The football Napoleons had met their Waterloo.

The lost opportunity for a night of football-fuelled bonhomie was so disappointing, it rendered them speechless. But not me. Still having my wits about me, I asked, "Do the rooms have TVs?" Success. The room had a TV if not an atmosphere, but we made the best of it with a couple of pints and a packet of crisps.

DAY 8

Date: Sunday 8 July

Start: 08:10 at Wye

Finish: 13:30 at Canterbury

Distance: 25.4km (15.9 miles)

Total: 248km (155 miles)

Daily average: 31.km (19.3 miles)

Minus Triathlete Pete and the portable caravan, we walked to Wye station and delightedly met up with Kath. A hiking pro, she too was ready to walk the Nile in a khaki-on-khaki combination, plus a large hat and a small backpack.

A few minutes later a taxi drew up and out stepped other friends: David, a former colleague of The Keeper, followed by Angelica, his beautiful Swedish wife, who was completely devoid of khaki. I do not think khaki is even in Angelica's multilingual vocabulary, let alone her wardrobe. Angelica had been meditating on the journey over and as she swung her long legs from the vehicle, an aura of serenity came with her. She smiled at us all. I hid my elephant legs.

Getting on with the task (and reassuring Angelica that we would stop to eat occasionally), we had a gorgeous day and saw the county of Kent at its finest. We walked through handsome beech woodland and alongside regiments of fruit trees bowing under the weight of their crop. Fields were flowering in a brilliant mosaic of colour, blue linseed, red poppies and golden corn.

Then, all too soon (for us anyway) we were walking through the city gate into Canterbury. David and Angelica left us to beat a hasty retreat to their hotel, food (for Angelica), a bath and rest being their priorities. Kath, The Keeper of the Maps and I headed towards the cathedral, the official start of the Via Francigena and our route to Rome.

The World Heritage cathedral welcomes over one million visitors a year. At Christ Church Gate, the entrance to the cathedral, we realised most of these visitors had decided to arrive that afternoon. There was quite a queue.

We stood in line, three weary backpack-clad individuals wafting the odour that comes from a day's walk in blistering sunshine. Not surprisingly, we were noticed, not only by our queue companions but also by a kindly official who asked, "Are you pilgrims?"

Now that is something that needed consideration. Were The Keeper and I pilgrims, and if so, in what sense? Up until then, I had not truly considered this question, yet there we were, standing at Canterbury Cathedral, with all our worldly goods on our backs, about to set off for the Eternal City. Unlike so many before us, we were not undertaking this journey as an act of religious devotion but for our own enjoyment. Apart from making us unusual, did that also make us pilgrims? Before I had time to engage the others in this philosophical conversation, they had both answered 'yes' and we were being led right past the envious queuing tourists, underneath the watchful eyes of the stone gargoyles and into the cathedral precinct. Kath, the daughter of a vicar, appeared to have no misgivings about her single day of walking equalling a pilgrimage, so I decided to not have any either.

Leaving Kath to wander around the cathedral, The Keeper and I found the official start of the Via Francigena, where we had our pilgrim passports stamped and were offered a blessing for a safe journey onwards.

We then took ourselves inside one of the oldest Christian structures in England and what had been one of the most important centres of pilgrimage in Medieval England, particularly after the infamous murder of Thomas Becket.

A filtered light, soothed of summer harshness by the vast stained-glass windows,

illuminated an architectural wonder. With its Norman arches, ribbed vaults and ornate stone tracery, the cathedral was a visionary overload. We tilted our heads to absorb the full enormity of the building and let our eyes dart from detail to detail. It was impossible to focus on one entity at a time such was the quantity and quality of the cathedral's embellishments.

In contrast to all there was to see, there was only an awed hush to hear. Visitors, made mute by the grandeur of faith and in acknowledgment of the significant chapters of England's history that had occurred within these very walls, walked in silence.

Gathering our thoughts, we went outside and looked up again. Even from an age of high-rise, it was impossible not to be awed by the cathedral's majesty. After a few minutes of contemplation, we were returned to the reality of our challenge by the constant presence of our backpacks. We were about to walk to Rome. A journey that others, from this very spot, had taken before us, including our 10th-century guide and mentor Sigeric the Serious.

What had Sigeric felt as he too had stood here? Had excitement and apprehension tingled through his bones as it was through mine? I looked at The Keeper. "Isn't it all amazing and exciting?" I asked, and followed up with, "What are you thinking?"

"That I need a shower," came the irreverent reply.

We said goodbye to Kath and headed to our hotel. Whilst The Keeper showered, I looked up the definition of a pilgrim. I found that as well as being a synonym for tourist, it can also be described as 'a person travelling to a place of particular personal interest'. I fell asleep that night content that The Keeper and I were indeed pilgrims.

DAY 9

Date: Monday 9 July

Start: 05:40 at Canterbury

Finish: 14:00 at Dover/Calais

Distance: 35.0km (21.9 miles)

Total: 283km (177 miles)

Daily average: 31.4km (19.6 miles)

When David and Angelica signed up for the 'Kent bit' of Home to Rome, they had not expected to find themselves in the foyer of their boutique hotel at 05.30. Yet, there they were to meet us. They had pulled themselves from the hotel's soft and downy bed, eased their tired and blistered feet into stiff boots and, abandoning any hope of a delicious breakfast, they were ready to be off. With enormous gratitude for these good friends, we moved out into the empty streets of Canterbury.

Without the clutter and noise of fellow tourists, we were able to enjoy the city centre. Shops, homes and restaurants that had served their community from the Middle Ages jostled for position alongside the High Street. Timber-framed buildings in their livery of black and white sat between the muscular stone of medieval buildings and the ornate brick detail of Victorian facades. An architectural disorder of charm. Built, lived in and hopefully loved by a succession of people ignorant of planning consultants or building regulations, these dwellings had nevertheless stood the test of time. They had afforded protection and income and in return witnessed the minutiae of local lives and the drama of national events.

We all had a touch of regret when we walked past the city wall, leaving Canterbury and its capsules of history behind us.

After putting away some miles but not any caffeine (much missed by our double-espresso-loving Angelica), we eventually caught our first glimpse of some white cliffs and the English Channel.

Angelica, we had discovered, rather like an elegant parking meter, needed feeding small amounts regularly. When we reached Guston, the idea of a pub lunch and a taxi back to Canterbury got the better of her. We left them to their well-deserved meal and trundled on to Dover where, using the honed skills of The Keeper of the Maps, we managed to find the passenger terminal for P&O Ferries.

As we entered the terminal building smiles creased our faces. There, lined up on P&O's finest plastic chairs, was the Folkestone arm of The Keeper's family, out in full to meet us.

We were just commencing the 'arms wide, air-kissing' family greeting when we were launched upon by a French pilgrim cunningly disguised as a gnome (smiley face, red hat, little shorts, big feet). This rather spoiled the moment and left me having to deal with the gnome.

Me: "Hello there, can I help you?"

Gnome: "Where did you get zee badge?"

Me: "What badge?"

Gnome: "Zee 'Ome to Rome badge. I have need of one."

So, I gave him one (a badge that is). He went away happy and also, apparently, walking from our house to Rome between 1 July and 15 September 2018.

We caught the ferry and watched from the deck as we left both family and England behind. We had made it this far and celebrated on board with the necessary cup of tea. By the time we reached Calais and our hotel, it had been a long day. However, the Brits were finally abroad. A fact that was illustrated perfectly when The Keeper leant out of the bedroom window and hung his laundry, for all to see, on the Holiday Inn flagpole.

ENGLISH CHANNEL
HOME
Canterbury
Dover
Calais
WE ARE HERE
Thérouanne
Arras
Péronne
Laon
Reims
Châlons-en-Champagne
Brienne-le-Château
Bar-Sur-Aube
Langres
Champlitte
Besançon
Lausanne
Montreux
Col du Grand-Saint-Bernard
Aosta
Ivrea
Pavia
Piacenza
Fidenza
Fornovo di Taro
Berceto
Pontremoli
Lucca
San Gimignano
Siena
Bolsena
ROMA
ADRIATIC SEA
BAY OF BISCAY
TYRRHENIAN SEA
N
E
S
W

DAY 10

Date: Tuesday 10 July

Start: 07:30 at Calais

Finish: 15:20 at Licques

Distance: 29.9km (18.7 miles)

Total: 313km (195 miles)

Daily average: 31.3km (19.5 miles)

Calais, bright and early and viewed on foot, caught us by surprise. It was charming and offered so much more than the ferry terminal we all know and do not love. The last of England's possessions on French soil, the port town was the evocation of the British seaside: municipal buildings were fronted by grand floral displays and shopping streets were hung with colourful bunting.

We found the local canal and followed it out of town, arriving at Guînes several hours later.

Canal-side walking is hard going on the body. The monotonous repetition on a flat surface is wearing on both the joints and feet. I needed a quick break, but unfortunately, I could not depend on The Keeper needing one, he rarely did. But he never said no to tea.

"Shall we stop for a drink?" I asked.

"Good idea," replied The Keeper and without looking, walked straight into the nearest bar. I might have got the question right but not the timing.

The bar had an immodest number of football flags and the heavy scent of 'eau de testosterone' wafting from the unshirted underarms of the all-male clientele. I noticed a game of pool stop mid pot as half a dozen of these customers turned in unison to stare at The Keeper entering their domain. The Keeper was oblivious. I hesitated outside. How would these burly locals view me, a walking turtle who asked for tea?

It could not have been more convivial. Bonjours were exchanged and hands were shaken, not just with one or two of the customers, oh no, but the entire gang. Once I had made my way around them all, I was desperately in need of both a chair and a drink. The Keeper, finally picking up the nuance of the situation, ordered a manly beer. I hesitantly and quietly put in my order for tea.

The barkeeper, a large man in a small singlet, moved into action and started searching cupboards. He was on his knees when he found the tea and on his toes, when he found a cup and saucer. The whole was triumphantly served to me on a tray which I accepted with delight.

Later that afternoon we stopped for tea again, this time in a quaint cafe with wonderful encaustic tiles and no armpits. It was my choice, a safe but disappointingly uneventful one.

We walked on to a small hamlet and our hotel for the night. A former mill, it still had the original water wheel working, right in the middle of the guest sitting room. As the wheel scooped and dropped its water, it left a soft mist hanging in the air. An oasis of plant life in pots, trugs and baskets filled the room and blossomed in the moisture-laden atmosphere.

It was a surprisingly successful room for the indifferent hotelier. Unless they had had the foresight to pack neoprene, damp armchairs are not an ideal place for guests to linger. Lingering, we realised, was discouraged. Booking us in for the night, the hotelier told us that dinner was served at 19:30 or not at all. We were in the dining room at 19:28.

DAY 11

Date: Wednesday 11 July

Start: 06:15 at Licques

Finish: 15:00 at Therouanne

Distance: 35.6km (22.3 miles)

Total: 348km (218 miles)

Daily average: 31.6km (19.8 miles)

By now we were used to creeping out of our hotels in the early hours, tiptoeing in our dainty walking boots down dimly lit hallways, and today was no exception. We left the slumbering guests to enjoy their *petit dejeuner* at precisely 08:30 and got on the road. Unfortunately, this set the theme for the entire day: rolling terrain but mostly on road.

The farmland we passed was bountiful, ripening crops in vast, commercial fields, but the villages told another story. Houses shuttered and left to fend for themselves were prevalent. Village centres were empty, desolate places left stranded by the loss of the agrarian lifestyle in favour of the urban one. In vain and increasing decay, the villages were left to sit in wait for their communities to return.

It took us five hours to find anything for breakfast, by which time we were desperate. On the trail, food is fuel, and we were running out of it. We finally came across a *boulangerie* with its lights on and crawled in, hungrily scanning the shelves as we did so.

A few baguettes were lined up behind the counter and within them I could just see three deliciously buttery croissants peeking out. I snuck a peak at The Keeper, wondering if he had also noticed them. He had, damn. We would have to share.

What was I thinking? Of course, we would share! 'Hunger makes a thief of any man', well not this woman. Not just yet anyway.

We bought the three croissants and a baguette from the proprietress and after a brief chat, we asked if the bar next door was open. The proprietress considered for a moment and replied that she thought it probably was.

We said au revoir and went next door. As we entered the bar through the street door, we noticed a side door open. Changing her apron, as well as her persona, the *boulangerie* madam entered.

"Bonjour," she said, as if meeting us for the first time.

The Keeper shot me a look that asked, *what am I supposed to say now?* Playing safe, he replied, "Bonjour," as if he did not know her from Adam.

Then she continued, "You have walked far...?"

We both looked at each other *From next door...?* we were thinking, but we could not bring ourselves to break the farce and ordered coffee instead.

Later that afternoon, struggling again to find anything open and badly in need of refuelling, we saw a distant *boucherie*. Falling in through the door with intent, we obviously looked half-starved and in need of a little pick-me-up. Unknown to us, when wrapping our order, the warm-hearted M. Boucher sneakily tucked an extra lump of saucisson in with our goodies. A kind and unnecessary act that touched us.

It was a long, hard slog for the rest of the day into Therouanne. I was close to exhaustion and The Keeper was close to frustration. England were playing again, and he could not find a bar to watch the game.

We were staying in a hostel that night and luckily, as before, they had a television. That is where our luck ended, though. It was not England's night; football fever, for The Keeper, was over.

DAY 12

Date: Thursday 12 July

Start: 06:50 at Therouanne

Finish: 15:15 at Houdain

Distance: 34.1km (21.3 miles)

Total: 382km (239 miles)

Daily average: 31.9km (19.9 miles)

Despite the disappointment of the night before, The Keeper was up and ready, his normal positive self. Striding out on a cloud of contentment, with a hum of happiness emanating from under his hat, he set a good pace. Until, that is, we met an embankment, fencing and a discrepancy between the charted path and real life. Consulting the maps together, a decisive and mutual decision was made, by The Keeper. We would cut across a field of ripening corn and make up time that way. My limbs wilted at the prospect of yet another assault course and a new pair of elephant legs. "Why, what's the hurry?" I asked.

"No hurry, it's just... efficient," came the reply. *Efficient, my eye*, I thought as I waded in amongst the five-feet-high corn stalks. When I caught up with him it would be more than humming that he heard from under that hat.

I emerged from the corn trail, surprisingly unscathed, to find the village of Estrée-Blanche and The Keeper, who was sitting down. He never wanted to sit, so why should he now? And then he asked me to also sit for a while. Where was the 'efficiency' in that! I was beginning to be far from amused and starting to show it when I was asked to 'quiet down and look up the road'.

Begrudgingly, I looked up the road and there I saw our twenty-year-old son and two of his mates, all wearing impish grins of mischievousness on their faces and all looking directly at me.

Off on their own summer adventure of 'driving a dubious car to Mongolia' they had decided to call by and surprise me. The Keeper had been in on it, trying to get me to the prearranged meeting spot on time. They were all exceedingly pleased with themselves and I was beside myself with happiness. I would have jumped up and down with joy, but the weight of the darned backpack kept me grounded, so instead I did a funny sort of 'wiggle in wonder'.

We exchanged hugs and more hugs and had food and drink thrust in our hands. All too soon though, with promises to keep in touch, the boys drove off, my darned backpack in their car. Their parting gift of delivering it to that night's hotel was the best present they could have given me. Thanks to them, I was pack free and felt as light as a feather. The Keeper, having grown protective of his few possessions, could not quite bring himself to part with them, even for a day.

Our hotel for the night was a splendid château in Gosnay. As we entered the gilded foyer, barely contained puzzlement swept across the faces of the polite employees.

"Will you be staying with us tonight?" tentatively asked the receptionist, trying not to wilt at the prospect.

When we confirmed we would, the overhearing concierge had a light-bulb moment. "Then this," he said, "must be yours," triumphantly holding aloft (but discreetly away from his body) my backpack.

A deep, luxurious bath metamorphosed us both from dirty misfits to harmless eccentrics. Off to dinner strode earth mother and, on her arm, with his not inconsiderable nose, curly hair and glasses, a dead ringer for Postman Pat on holiday.

TO
ROME

cool earth
Y412 JRP

DAY 13

Date: Friday 13 July

Start: 08:15 at Houdain

Finish: 15:15 at Arras

Distance: 30.3km (18.9 miles)

Total: 413km (258 miles)

Daily average: 31.7km (19.8 miles)

I was not going to miss the opportunity of a sumptuous breakfast served in an equally sumptuous dining room, and thankfully, (after it was pointed out to him) neither was The Keeper. Deliciously full, we started out at the indulgent hour of 08:15 and headed for Houdain.

A once-thriving coal mining area employing over twenty thousand workers, the town consisted of hundreds of rows of neat brick terraced houses, former homes of the miners and their families. The Bruary Mining Company had created and dominated the community since opening its first mine in 1852. But it had left a mining legacy in desolation, with little employment or future when it closed its last pit in 1980.

Now, it seemed, the town was slowly regenerating. The cafe and the bakery were open for business and the town had a hopeful style about it, a bohemian chic *Coronation Street*.

Once out of the town, the countryside tracks gave us a pleasant day, popping us in and out of small woodlands. The soft, forgiving carpet of the woodland undergrounds felt as good under our boots as a thick Persian carpet under bare feet. Hard, fatigue-making road walking had been a feature of France so far. With each softer, bouncier step we felt a hedonistic glee of simple pleasure.

By early afternoon we could see the enormous ruins of the 18th-century abbey of Mont St Eloi on the skyline. Located on the ridge north of the city of Arras, it had been a distinct landmark for the soldiers based in this area during WWI. The abbey became our own landmark for much of the afternoon.

We walked into Arras as the day was ending and the city was coming to life. Shops were closing, office workers were hurrying home and the first of the spruced tourists, fresh from their hotel showers, were heading towards aperitifs. We were completely at odds with our environment, shrugging off the bemused looks of passers-by as we trudged along. Finally, having checked into our hotel (no, we did not have a car, nor luggage and yes, we did have a reservation), we too spruced ourselves and ventured out.

Most of Arras was lost in WWI. Heavy bombardments had reduced it to rubble, taking not only its principal buildings but ninety-five per cent of its houses. Whether to dispel trauma or evoke past glories, the French had passed a law in 1919 ruling that war-damaged ancient monuments should be rebuilt. Through grit, determination, national and international funding, Arras had painstakingly rebuilt itself.

We sat, enjoying a beer and our surroundings, in the Place des Héros, a monument to this reconstruction. 155 Baroque-style houses gloriously lined three sides of a cobbled square, with the town hall majestically occupying the fourth side. In replication of the original, each of the Flemish-style houses were on sandstone pilasters that formed an arcade at street level. The facades, topped with traditional Flemish curved rooflines, were either of brick or a white stone and rendered with colours that had softened over the years. As the sun eased, the square took on a pleasing hue of architectural harmony.

Locals and visitors alike filled the square with happy chatter and the clink of glasses, oblivious, perhaps, to the devastation and hard work that had gone before them. But did that matter? I think not. The square was meant for how it was now being enjoyed.

We sat back in the perfect backdrop with a sense of contentment and achievement. We had reached Arras, our first French milestone, and it felt so very good to have done so.

DAY 14

Date: Saturday 14 July

Start: 07:15 at Arras

Finish: 14:15 at Bapaume

Distance: 28.1km (17.6 miles)

Total: 441km (275 miles)

Daily average: 31.5 km (19.7 miles)

On our way out of Arras, we passed through the suburb of Beaurains. Beside the road was a WWI cemetry, the first, of what were to be many such cemeteries. We stopped to pay our respects and walked up and down the rows of headstones. The cemetery, a British one, was immaculate: neat, clean and planted with flowering shrubs. Each headstone bore the name, division, rank, date of death and often the age of the young man buried beneath.

We could not stand amongst these rows of sorrow, stone documents of sacrifice, and not be affected. The Keeper walked ahead, his head bowed. My thoughts turned to our own son and his friends enjoying their freedom on the open road, and then, with a sadness that comes from deep within, returned to those boys buried beneath me. Tears welled up in my eyes and overflowed, my handkerchief becoming damper with every row.

In the silence that comes from reverence, we collected ourselves and headed out into the countryside. It was to be a day of contrasts as today was 14 July, Bastille Day, and a time for communities to gather. Village after village was opening its hall in celebration. Banners and bunting had been hung and tables placed under trees, weighted down with the delights of local kitchens. The village elders sat chatting in the shade whilst the youngsters excitedly ran around them. And in the midst of it all, we were waved to as we passed by.

C.W. SWAIN
J. PARRY

One of the features of rural France, and in this part of France in particular, is the number of roadside crosses and crucifixes. Often quite substantial, they are found at intersections or village boundaries and were traditionally used as way-markers by travellers. Occasionally, instead of a cross, there is a simple chapel. At a particularly hot and shadeless part of the day we came across a perfect example of a roadside chapel. It was small, just large enough for two people, with a tiled roof, white painted walls, and a black and white tiled floor. Grateful for its cool shelter, we went in and found it had been furnished for us, as Via Francigena pilgrims. There was a tiny bench to rest on and a sign that told us 'Cantorbery' was 220km to the right and Rome 1720km to the left. There was also a shelf with a pilgrimage book to sign.

This was the first book of its type that we had come across on the Via Francigena. On any trail, these record books are of interest as they are the notice boards, recording past and present travellers, news and snippets of information. We signed and dated our own names below the last such entry, two other English hikers who were a few days ahead of us.

Back on the road, our afternoon was a tediously long one and we arrived in Bapaume footsore, hot and weary. We were following in the footsteps of Sigeric the Serious who, presumably like me, would have been dead beat at times. Yet the poor man had still managed to break out a quill and parchment each night and faithfully record the day's details. I only wish the 21st century scribes, sitting comfortably in front of their screens, had been as diligent when they compiled our Via Francigena guidebook. We were often walking much longer distances than those stated in the guide, and it had been those published distances that The Keeper had used to create our detailed (but now inaccurate) spreadsheet. Cumulatively small discrepancies on their part created exhausting days for us. Lines of detail were omitted; whole villages and stretches of road had been missed; straight lines between points had been used to calculate distances, ignoring the land contours that we could not. The extra six hard and unwanted miles to reach Bapaume that hot afternoon had been testament to their imprecision.

Later that evening, in the hotel's restaurant, I overheard an English family comment that they were 'a stone's throw' from Calais. A stone's throw! *You might be,* I thought, *but we are four long days away from Calais.*

This then caused me to reflect on our journey so far. Walking is less efficient (those land contours again) than other methods, granted. But this slow and intimate travel has one great advantage; you see the detail. Speeding along in a metal box on wheels, you get the bigger picture, but you miss the nuances. We had chatted to the locals and received their kindness; we had walked through the woodlands they valued and beside the fields they farmed. We had seen the graves of their dead and smelt the promise on their land at the dawn of a new day.

I shared my idealised thoughts, enhanced by the help of a glass of Burgundy, with The Keeper. To his huge relief, I did not share them with the English family on the next table. The last thing they wanted was an enthusiastic earth mother looming in telling them to abandon their car, tramp the baked earth and lift their noses to the smells of the Pas-de -Calais. No, all they wanted was dessert.

DAY 15

Date: Sunday 15 July

Start: 06:30 at Bapaume

Finish: 12:40 at Péronne

Distance: 28.8 km (18.0 miles)

Total: 469km (293 miles)

Daily average: 31.3km (19.6 miles)

We left Bapaume at 'beat the heat' o'clock and headed for Péronne. It was another tough day of relentless heat and thirst. No matter how much we drank, our bodies asked for more. When we eventually arrived, zombie-like, in Péronne, we had no physical choice but to head straight to a bar and a litre of ice-cold water. We sat in silence until the water had been absorbed by enough body parts to permit function. Then we went in search of our hotel.

We found it beside the gateway of the Port de Bretagne, the ancient official way into Britain and Flanders. If there was ever a masterclass on how to run a guest house, Laetitia, our hostess, would be top of it. She had turned an interesting 1930's house into a haven for the traveller. It was faultless.

Later, together with most of the population of Péronne, The Keeper and I headed to the bars in the town square and the big match. France was playing Croatia in the final of the World Cup. All ages from the pram up were there, all sporting the tricolour and all supporting their nation's heroes. When the final whistle blew, Péronne exploded with the all-consuming energy of the winning side. People whooped, cheered and cried. Fireworks were set off whilst a parade of cars drove round and round the square with a cavalcade of flags and noise accompanying them. This sheer joyous fun lasted far longer than we did.

FRA

DAY 16

Date: Monday 16 July

Start: 08:15 at Péronne

Finish: 13:30 at Etreillers

Distance: 25.6km (16.0 miles)

Total: 495km (309 miles)

Daily average: 30.9km (19.3 miles)

With the prospect of only seventeen miles ahead of us, we decided to stay for Laetitia's breakfast. And thank the heavenly stars that we did.

Her dining table that morning was a perfect display of encapsulated deliciousness. Omelette, bacon, warm bread, granola, lemon cake, *pain perdu*, yoghurt, fresh fruit, honey and freshly squeezed orange juice were beautifully laid upon it. It was the sublime highlight of what was to be a day of diminishing returns.

Out into the countryside once more, we turned off a baking road into a cool, green tunnel of trees, dappled with dark pools of water. *How charming*, we foolishly thought. *Fresh meat in the lair,* thought the local community of bloodsuckers, who had learnt the art of flying in packs.

It became an inescapable tunnel of torment as horseflies and mosquitoes lay siege to any parts of our bodies they could reach. We batted and swiped ourselves and each other for a whole kilometre until, thirty-three bites later (The Keeper kept count, of course), we emerged into the safety of dry sunshine and heat.

We arrived in Etreillers itchy and desperate to shower the day away, but we were too early to book into our accommodation. The local tabac was boarded up, and there did not appear to be much else in the village square apart from the church. "Stay here with the packs and I'll take a look around," announced The Keeper. When he returned, empty handed, he found me fast asleep in the only shade available, on the church steps.

Moving me off, like some foundling, to a park bench behind the church, The Keeper announced he was off again, as he had noticed a sign for another shop. I put all we owned around me, made a pillow from my fleece and fell asleep again. From foundling to bag lady in three minutes.

Returning from a mini supermarket with an arm full of goodies, The Keeper nudged me awake. "Are you all right?" he asked, concerned. "You seem to be sleeping a lot."

I rubbed my eyes and thought about it. This was our sixteenth day on the road in blazing heat and we had walked 500km. "I'm just a bit tired," I answered.

"Oh good," he replied. "For a minute there, I thought it was something you might have done."

Having eaten our snacks and applied yet more antihistamine, we went in search of our B&B.

We found an old stone building with its back to the road and no obvious door. We were just scratching our heads, wondering how to make ourselves known, when we heard an '*ello* from a string-vested, stubbly man leaning out of a window.

He confirmed we were to stay with him that night. He also confirmed that the small unnumbered door on the corner, the door behind the two fallen motorbikes resting on the bed of weeds, was indeed the way in. As there was no other accommodation within walking distance, we hesitantly stepped over the bikes and went in. Things did not look good.

And they were not. In the space of twenty four hours, we sampled both ends of the hospitality spectrum.

DAY 17

Date: Tuesday 17 July

Start: 05:30 at Etreillers

Finish: 12:00 at Tergnier

Distance: 29.6km (18.5 miles)

Total: 525km (328 miles)

Daily average: 30.9km (19.3 miles)

We were up and out of chez dodgy vest before the sun had risen. Eating stale bread rolls, boiled eggs and a bit of cheese (found lurking in the bottom of The Keeper's bag), we wistfully recollected the breakfast of the day before. We were not disheartened, however, and pressed on with another day on the trail.

As well as being The Keeper of the Maps, the same lovable chap held the position of The Keeper of the Office, often taking calls and answering emails as we walked along. He thought he was rather good at it until this multi tasking brought him up short.

We were a few hours into our day, and I was plodding along, head down, minding my own business, when I came upon a heap of Keeper on the grass.

"What are you doing down there?" I asked.

"I don't know," came the stunned reply.

"Well, I don't want to sit on the grass beside this road, so why are you?" I asked with my usual supply of charm and patience.

"My head stopped but my feet didn't, and here I am," he answered.

Hmmm, I thought, looking around. "That's because you have just walked into a road sign."

"Well, who put that there?"

I was going to venture that it was probably the department of transport but decided to keep mute. I did suggest, however, that long emails were written in shorter sections in future.

Finally, and without further incident, we arrived in Tergnier, our Via Francigena destination, but not our home for the night. Tergnier is the French equivalent to Crewe, but without the sights and in our case, without any accommodation to offer. We caught a train to St Quentin and stayed there for the night, catching the 05:51 back again the next day.

DAY 18

Date: Wednesday 18 July

Start: 06:15 at Tergnier

Finish: 14:15 at Laon

Distance: 36.3km (22.7 miles)

Total: 561km (351 miles)

Daily average: 31.2km (19.5 miles)

From the train station, we walked for an hour through the non-descript suburbs of Tergnier. In unspoken agreement, we hunkered down and got on with the job of putting the necessary, but not particularly enjoyable, miles behind us.

As another day of heat and road-walking wore on, we gradually left behind the open flat land, with its ever-present company of wind turbines, and came across the occasional, but very welcome, woodland.

Our destination was Laon, an ancient hilltop town in the historic district of Picardy, now part of the Hauts-de-France. We first noticed Laon in the far-off distance and even then, it dominated its landscape. We could see the outline of the town on the crest of its own hilltop, a Disney silhouette against the deep blue sky. As we snaked our way across the landscape, the town grew in majesty until, at mile nineteen, it loomed directly above us. And then the reality of what was to come hit me like a slap from a wet salmon. My hotel for the night, my shower and my dinner were all above me. My last mile was going to be a vertical one.

Thankfully, this rather belated epiphany occurred outside a handily positioned cafe stocked with ice-cold drinks. Refreshed and refuelled, I exited the cafe with as much determination as a khaki turtle on a sugar rush can manage.

Off I went, leaving The Keeper to follow in the dust of my departure, shaking his head in resigned bewilderment. Up and up we climbed, over gravel, earth and cobbles. My walking poles clicking those cobbles like knitting needles on speed. Finally, and with little dignity, we reached the top and caught our breath, only to have it taken again by the view before us.

In all directions, as far as our eyes could see, were fields, roads, railways; an exceptional panorama of the plains of Picardy. We stood and soaked it in, then with some regret, we tore ourselves away from the view and turned to Laon itself. What we discovered was a retirement home for ancient buildings. There are eighty listed buildings in the town centre alone, a wonder of medieval architecture.

The 12th century Notre-Dame de Laon, an elder to the Notre Dame de Paris, is one of the principal works of wonder. We went to see the Gothic masterpiece and stood in awe, our eyes raised up to its looming facade.

A deep connection to those who had stood there before me entered my consciousness. It was a connection, not with the vividly dressed tourists, smelling of scented chemicals and viewing the cathedral through the sequential seconds of their camera shutters, but with the unassuming figures of past pilgrims. The individuals who, like me, had kept the cathedral in their sights for hours, who had walked towards it, seeing it as a place of sanctuary and shelter. Those people who must have stood where I was standing, in awe and thankfulness to have made it this far.

DAY 19

Date: Thursday 19 July

Start: 05:55 at Laon

Finish: 12:20 at Corbeny

Distance: 29.3km (18.3 miles)

Total: 590km (369 miles)

Daily average: 31.1km (19.4 miles)

At 05.30 we were both bent over our packs, choosing to carry them in our arms rather than on our backs where they might knock something. Like burglars with acute osteoporosis, we were creeping quietly along the corridors of our hotel, when we came across a problem. The front door was locked. Scratching our heads in dismay, we looked around the reception area and then around the reception desk where we discovered a buzzer.

I looked at The Keeper, should we buzz the buzzer? Would it open the door, call through to someone on duty or, God forbid, set off an alarm? Two of the three were in our favour so I tentatively pressed and waited for all hell to break loose. Nothing happened. We waited and still nothing happened. No alarm, no click of the door lock, no one came.

I buzzed again and we waited again. Still nothing happened.

Now, The Keeper is a results-focused individual who is not easily distracted from his goal. His goal that morning was to exit the hotel early. But what if he could not get out through the door?

"I am going to look for an open window," he whispered.

"You can't," I replied in a hushed voice. "We can't climb out of a hotel window."

Adopting selective hearing, The Keeper started looking for an unlocked window and found one in the dining room. As I entered the dining room, he was happily engaged in rearranging tables and manipulating a sash window. "We can't do this," I repeated in a desperate whisper. For an answer, I was handed a backpack and told to hand it back to him through the window.

The Keeper was just straddling the window, one leg in and one leg out, when he realised the ground on the other side of the window was further down than the floor on the hotel side. Ouch, that did not look comfortable.

"What is it you do?" boomed a voice at my shoulder, shooting me out of my skin. The manager had appeared.

"What is it you do?" I replied, hoping to distract him from the 6ft 4inch tall English man who was now uncomfortably straddling his window.

"What if there had been a fire?" I continued. "The front door is locked, so we would not have been able to get out."

Not appreciating the question from the English woman with her rosbif partner, who was doing something inappropriate with the window ledge, he answered. "You 'ave zee buzzer, you buzz me."

"I buzz you. I buzz you two times, but the buzzer didn't buzz," I replied.

Puffing out his chest with indignation and bringing a forefinger into play, he quipped, "Zee buzzer always buzzes. I think, madame, zatt you (pointing the finger) try buzz off without pay."

With difficulty, The Keeper withdrew his leg so that both limbs were again hotel-side of the window and, in a high-pitched voice, verified our prepayment. Satisfied that the two escapologists were peculiar but not dishonest, the manager hastily opened the front door and pushed us out, closing it firmly behind us. We collected ourselves, not daring to catch the other's eye, but when we heard the thud of the sash window also being closed, it was too much. With tears of barely contained laughter rolling down our cheeks, we made as dignified an exit along the street as we were able.

The rest of the day was spent in rolling countryside all the way to our destination, Corbeny. As we approached the town, we saw the uplifting site of our first champagne vines, but right in front of them was the more sombre site of a war memorial. We learnt that the town's strategic position had caused it to be the site of many Western Front battles. In one horrific offensive, the Second Battle of the Aisne in April 1917, several hundred thousand men had been killed. We stood, immobilised by disbelief, and looked out across the fields. *It was time, just a slip of time,* I thought, *that allows me to look out over champagne vines, my family safe, when others in another time have looked out across carnage.*

I reached for The Keeper's hand and quietly, we went to find our hotel.

DAY 20

Date: Friday 20 July

Start: 05:25 at Corbeny

Finish: 14:00 at Reims

Distance: 38.0km (23.8 miles)

Total: 628km (393 miles)

Daily average: 31.4km (19.6 miles)

Having established the night before that the front door of the hotel would definitely be open, we left as the rooster crowed, ready for a long day. It was pleasant walking with the added variety of undulation. We were on tracks mostly, across fields and through some woodland.

With twenty miles finally behind us, we walked into Reims. I was tired but keeping it together, which is more than I can say of my boots. Objecting to all I was putting them through, they had simply fallen apart at the seams.

It was clear that my boots would need replacing but neither of us could face that task before we cleaned up. At the end of every day, we had established a routine. We washed ourselves, we washed our kit and we (well, me mostly) napped.

To do this politely, we needed a room, so we found our hotel and, by not blending in with the tourist norm, we received our keys spectacularly quickly.

We were waiting for the lift to whisk us away to a shower and a soft bed when we were joined by a young member of staff. "You take the lift," I said. "We will wait for the next." But his training and youth would not hear of it, and he assured us that we could all fit into the small space. The journey up to our floor was painfully slow and painfully polite,

each of us ignoring the fact that two of us in that lift wafted an odour and one of us wafted regret. He had received some life training on us.

Cleansed and lift-respectable, our next mission was to replace the failing boots. The Keeper identified an out-of-town Decathlon; I ordered a taxi, and before we knew it, we were on our way. Well, nearly on our way. We spent a few minutes parked at the curb confirming, and reconfirming, our chosen destination. The taxi driver, whilst polite, was confused. A Decathlon store is not the usual tourist destination in Reims. When we explained that we had walked from England and needed new boots, his look of astonishment was delightful. Understanding the importance of the mission, he focused on getting us there with time to spare.

Warning The Keeper that to get it right may take some time, I found the women's aisle of walking boots. Some fifteen minutes later, I had moved my search to the men's aisle. Some fifteen minutes after that, I was not in a good place: I, like my boots, was beginning to fall apart at the seams. At this point, The Keeper decided to focus on his emails, which was not a good decision, not a good decision at all. An opinion I might have shared with him.

Recognising that input was needed quickly, The Keeper speedily scanned the upper shelves for inspiration and a contribution. "Try these then," he announced triumphantly, whilst lifting down a pair of brown, beefy, men's boots and offering them to me as if I should be pleased.

At that point, I was no Cinderella, but I did slip them on, and they did fit like a glove. With relief and a little princely smugness, The Keeper headed for the till.

We celebrated later that evening with a glass or two of champagne and a bottle of Rully. We had walked to Reims, after all.

DAY 21

Date: Saturday 21 July

Start: 07:25 at Reims

Finish: 15:00 at Bouzy

Distance: 35.3km (22.1 miles)

Total: 664km (415 miles)

Daily average: 31.6km (19.7 miles)

We could not leave the city without first visiting the Notre-Dame de Reims, famous for being the traditional location for the coronation of the kings of France. The present building was begun in 1211, although a cathedral has stood on its site since 401. Its facade is laden with statues and embellishments, 2,300 of them the explanatory leaflet told us. It is as if each generation had felt compelled to add to the cathedral's glory but had only succeeded in weighing it down in fuss and workload. The building apparently is in a constant state of repair.

Keen to get underway after our cathedral delay, we each bought a single *pain-au-raisin* as a stopgap until we found a more substantial breakfast. In our haste, we had forgotten that our breakfast hopes had been dashed before, and we should have prepared for them to be dashed again and bought in bulk.

We left the city of Reims by following the Aisne canal out of town. It was Saturday, and the residents of Reims were about their exercise. Cyclists, joggers and fellow walkers wished us *bon courage* as we passed them by.

The feeling of bonhomie, born in the city, evaporated as we walked further into the countryside. The villages and hamlets that we walked through contained beautiful houses but little evidence of community. Our hopes of finding an open shop or bar and replenishing the calories we were using were let down time and time again.

We were firstly aiming for Verzenay, in the heart of Champagne country. To get to it, we walked through miles of immaculately tended vines, the name of the vineyard that owned them proprietarily placed at the end of each row. We were in beautiful Bacchus country, but whilst the god of wine and intoxication obviously drank, he surely did not eat. We arrived in Verzenay, having walked the best part of six hours on just a single pastry.

We made our way through the village, getting more and more despondent; nothing selling or serving food was open. Eventually, we came across a *boulangerie* that was disinterestedly offering baguettes and soggy bottomed quiches. With relief and lethargy, I leant against the wall whilst The Keeper went in to round up as many soggy bottoms as he could carry. Picking me up from my wallflower position, he helped me across the road and parked my bottom onto a low wall. We ate with abandon.

Gradually, the world came back into focus, and I realised that we were surrounded by some of the best Champagne houses in the world. Whilst I enviously watched air-conditioned cars bringing potential customers to their doors, I wondered who was having the better time. The Keeper and I sitting on our dodgy wall, snuffling our lunch out of paper bags and drinking warm water from our bottles or the visitors to the Grandes Marques, tasting nectar from long-stemmed glasses? No contest, I reasoned, they were.

Later that afternoon (and after a few more miles of vines), we arrived in the appropriately named village of Bouzy. Our hosts for the night were welcoming, and our room was delightful. They did not, however, offer an evening meal, so I asked where the nearest restaurant was.

"Very near, just a kilometre, the other side of the village," was the disappointing answer.

The restaurant might be near in a car but not when your legs are spent, and your choice of transport is either boots or sandals. But as it was the nearest restaurant, we set off and arrived at its door, which was closed. Their opening hours were nowhere to be seen, so we knocked.

"You are too early, go away," was the greeting thrown at us from behind a slightly opened door.

"When do you open?" we asked, quite reasonably we thought. We were obviously wrong.

"When we are ready, around thirty minutes from now," came the reply.

"We are on foot. Can we sit and wait in your garden?"

"No."

The door was closed on us. We looked at each other in astonishment and then indignation. We would rather starve than give them business. Well, perhaps not starve, not twice in one day. Then the Keeper had a moment of enlightenment. He had noticed a mini market, although trickily not its opening times. We trudged warily back to the village and found the shop was not only open but packed with local goodies. What a relief.

Our arms full of supper, we returned to the guest house where, noticing our situation, the owner kindly set a table in her garden. Under the protection of an ancient olive tree, we enjoyed a delightful dinner, a delicious bottle of champagne and the knowledge that we had not given the restaurant the business it did not deserve.

ENGLISH CHANNEL
HOME
Canterbury
Dover
Calais
Thérouanne
Arras
Péronne
Laon
WE ARE HERE
MAP
Reims
Châlons-en-Champagne
Brienne-le-Château
Bar-Sur-Aube
Langres
Champlitte
Besançon
Lausanne
Montreux
Col du Grand-Saint-Bernard
Aosta
Ivrea
Piacenza
Pavia
Fidenza
Fornovo di Taro
Berceto
Pontremoli
Cucca
San Gimignano
Siena
Bolsena
ADRIATIC SEA
BAY OF BISCAY
ROMA
TYRRHENIAN SEA
N
W
E
S

DAY 22

Date: Sunday 22 July

Start: 08:15 at Bouzy

Finish: 13:30 at Châlons-en-Champagne

Distance: 27.4km (17.1 miles)

Total: 691km (432 miles)

Daily average: 31.4km (19.6 miles)

The breakfast table was so laden with delicious morsels, arranged upon equally delicious china, that removing anything between the display and the plate felt like an act of vandalism. We soon warmed to the task, however, and enjoyed a meal to rival Laetitia's in Péronne. Eventually, and contentedly, we rolled our way out of the village, following a straight road to Conde-sur-Marne. From there, we spent the rest of the day walking along the Canal Latéral à la Marne.

As the canal was tree-lined, it was a day of slightly tunnelled vision but also a day with shade, which gave us a much-needed respite from the heat and, for that, we were grateful.

Châlons-en-Champagne, despite being only a quarter of the size of Reims, is the capital of the department of Marne. This is due, in the large part, to having the good fortune of staying loyal to the crown during the Wars of Religion. It has a smattering of buildings of note, including a cathedral, but the town's real charm is in the ancient half-timbered houses and stores that line its streets.

Determined never to be more than a backpack away from a calorie again, we went to explore the town and to search out provisions. At home, we try to avoid single-use plastic, and we were determined to keep this up on the road. Perhaps my earth mother outfit was appropriate after all.

Fresh eggs that came in cardboard boxes were always a treasured find. Boiled and tucked away in a pocket, they were useful protein bombs pre-packed in their own biodegradable shells. Priceless.

On the road, apart from stuffing the odd bit of cheese into a bread roll, transforming fresh eggs to boiled eggs was our only other culinary achievement. We would pop our eggs and water into the hotel room kettle and switch it on. After reaching a boil and switching itself off, the kettle would be left alone for an hour or so. The tricky bit for both of us was to remember to retrieve the 'cooked to perfection' eggs. We needed them more than the next, surprised, guest of the hotel room did.

Whilst our Châlons-en-Champagne eggs were poaching in their water, we went to dinner. Ordering a pre-dinner drink, I put in a request for *un diablo violette*. "Are you sure?" asked The Keeper in surprise.

"Yes," I replied, realising my subconscious had ordered for me. I had seen someone drinking one across the bar and I was suddenly transported back to the UK. Knowing my peculiar fondness for Parma Violets, our children would often gift me the little packets of sweets as tokens of love. I was inadvertently ordering memories of home, in a glass.

DAY 23 & 24

Date: Monday 23 & Tuesday 24 July

Start: 07:15 at Châlons-en-Champagne

Finish: 14:30 at Donnement

Distance: 58.7km (36.5 miles)

Total: 750km (469 miles)

Daily average: 31.2km (19.5 miles)

The next two days were spent on a Roman road, and it felt like *The Road to Perdition*. Hot, hot and hotter still.

The road varied in its surface between chalk, gravel and tarmac. But it did not vary in its starkness. There was no shade; there were no villages, nothing, *rien*, just one long, open road across big, open fields.

By mid-morning on the first day, we were desperate just to sit somewhere, anywhere that gave us a bit of respite from the heat. We found a small field hedge, beside which was a ditch. Crawling in like two feral animals, we sat in the dry dirt with our knees up and looked at each other.

"What exactly are we doing?" I asked.

"We are walking from Home to Rome," replied The Keeper with all the empathy of a plastic potty, which, if I had one, I might have thrown at him. But then, dryly, he added, "But I'll hedge my bets we will come out from under this one and make it." A one-liner that caught the moment, causing a slight, but only slight, smile to escape my dry lips. Five minutes later, The Keeper pulled me to my feet and we pressed on.

The only company we had was the occasional farmer passing by on his tractor. If we met the tractor on a chalk stretch, we were done for. The dust cloud following in its wake would engulf us, covering us in a fine white flour. After a couple of these passings we ended up white from hat to boots, feeling like two bakery products ready for the oven: a baguette and a beignet slowly being cooked on the road to perdition.

By the second day, the giant wind turbines, sentinels that punctuated our barren landscape, had become friends. We had learnt that at their bases, they had a few steps. If a turbine was near the road, and if the sun was in the right position, these steps were in the sliver of shade cast from the turbine's slender body. When all the 'ifs' worked, we collapsed gratefully on to those steps.

By the second afternoon, we had finally reached the tiny village of Corbeil and the end of perdition. We walked into the small village in a state of relief and exhaustion, desperately looking for fresh water and a bench. We could not see either, but we could see a patch of shaded grass beside the church gravestones. With no other choice, we collapsed onto the hard earth and slept.

Waking from our siesta, we were still in need of water, so we knocked at the door of the nearest house. In answer to our request, we were given a key and a kind smile. The key was to the parish hall beside which we had slept. Inside, we found two cot beds, a bathroom, water and coffee facilities. This small village had put together a haven for tired pilgrims. If only they had thought to add a sign.

That evening, when we were in a bar celebrating having beaten the road to perdition, but still trying to quench the day's thirst, we had a conversation with some men who had spent their day fishing.

"Did you catch anything?" I asked.

"No, have you walked far?" they asked. In response to my answer, we were bought another round of drinks.

DAY 25

Date: Wednesday 25 July

Start: 07:15 at Donnement

Finish: 12:15 at Brienne-le-Château

Distance: 24.7km (15.4 miles)

Total: 774km (484 miles)

Daily average: 31.0km (19.4 miles)

As sleep left me and I came into consciousness, my stomach scrunched. It was light and yet we were not on the road! Panic, panic, panic. And then I remembered, we only had 12 miles to walk today. Joy, joy, joy.

The morning's walk had touches of field, woodland, lake and a good amount of shade, glorious shade.

We arrived at our hotel, in Brienne-le-Château, with the temperature in the mid-thirties and rising. We had a quick lunch and, as we were in an attic bedroom with no air conditioning, a sweaty nap. Once rested, we ventured out into the town to enjoy our half-day holiday.

Brienne-le-Château, in its more glorious days, had been the centre of the medieval county of Brienne. Nowadays, it is an inconsequential town with a traffic-heavy central road and a marketing-savvy council. The town had three claims to fame that it diligently publicised.

Firstly, that it had hosted Napoleon for a few years as a military student; secondly, it is overlooked by a huge château; and thirdly, it hosts a sauerkraut festival in September. Too early for the dubious delights of sauerkraut, we sought out the other two attractions.

We got halfway up the hill to the château when our path was barred by fencing and a sign announcing its closure. Peering through the fencing, we could just see a flanked symmetrical facade of pale stone and fenestration, topped by a slate roof that met in peaks. It was a sublime epitome of French castle architecture and had once been beautiful, rightfully deserving of its colloquial name 'Le petit Versailles de l'Aube'. But now, it sat in a rather sad and derelict state, like some grand old lady, held together by scaffolding, goodwill and much in need of a facelift. I had some sympathy.

Undeterred, we trotted off to find Napoleon, but whilst we had eaten lunch, he had closed for the day. So much for our holiday. We retreated to a bar and caught up with our paperwork.

Returning to the hotel for dinner, we heard English accents coming from the table behind us. Turning to greet the two owners of the accents, I had a sudden realisation: they were fellow pilgrims.

What alerted me, who knows? Perhaps it was their healthy glow or perhaps, and more likely, it was my memory of the two names we had seen in the chapel's pilgrim book eleven days earlier.

"What brings you to Brienne-le-Château?" I asked.

With a hint of pride, carefully played down by a helping of British modesty, the answer "We walked here," was returned. They both then looked at us, waiting for our expected expression of surprise and admiration. We obviously did not exude a hint of healthy hiker glow, or they might have been forewarned of my answer.

Naughtily, I could not resist nonchalantly replying "Yeah, so did we."

We spent the rest of the dinner happily swapping trail-tales and general chit-chat across the tables. Except for the French gnome, James and Julie were the first Via Francigena pilgrims that we had come across.

DAY 26

Date: Thursday 26 July

Start: 05:20 at Brienne-le-Château

Finish: 12:10 at Bar-sur-Aube

Distance: 30.8km (19.3 miles)

Total: 805km (503 miles)

Daily average: 31.0km (19.4 miles)

We emerged from the hotel into the cool gloom of the early morning and walked through a Brienne-le-Château hushed by sleep. One behind the other, we quietly passed through the town centre to its urban fringe and from there to the countryside and the grey light of pre-dawn.

We were in open fields when the sun rose from the edge of the land, casting its energy outwards, turning the grey light to a golden one. We paused to savour the ancient wonder, a bestowed privilege that at that moment felt like it was ours alone.

Our first destination was Dienville, a lovely *Ville Fleuri* made even lovelier by the fact that its tabac opened at 06:30. We were outside the door at 06:28 counting down the minutes until it opened. Refreshed and refuelled with coffee and pastries, we walked on to Dolancourt.

Dolancourt is an equally attractive village with neatly pointed stone houses and an enthusiastic flower committee. Rather surprisingly, it also has a theme park attached to it, Nigloland. We were passed by car after car of apprehensive parents driving animated children. As the roller coasters worked their magic, the undulating sounds of exhilaration and relief, thrills and chills filled the air. It was as if we were sharing a pretty Cotswold village with the soundtrack of a big dipper on loop.

We walked on through to midday, the terrain improving on the previous week as we did so; some undulation providing interest and more patches of woodland providing a reprieve from the heat. Stopping to chat with an elderly lady in her front garden, we were asked, "Vous allez à Rome?" *Ha ha*, I thought, our first recognition as *pelerins*. She had obviously noticed our healthy hiker glow. But no, she had simply read our backpack badges.

In Bar-sur-Aube, we were delighted to find that our hotel had a pool, a small one but a pool all the same. The fact that our packing list had not allowed for the extra weight of a swimsuit was a minor issue The Keeper was happy to overlook; I found it a little harder to do so. Deciding that skinny dipping was out of the question, I looked to my only other resource, my netherwear. Much washed and designed for durability rather than fun, they were a world away from Victoria's Secret, but they were going to have to be my secret. Underlining my prudishness by asking The Keeper to wear something, anything, we wrapped the hotel towels around us and snuck down to the pool, thankfully empty of other guests.

Whilst I slipped in discreetly, The Keeper jumped in with wanton abandon, rising to the surface with a roar: Neptune, in underpants.

Back in our room, The Keeper was checking the spreadsheet when a whoop of triumph left his lips. He put 'I'm Gonna Be' by The Proclaimers on his phone and the immortal lines about walking 500 miles sang out across our room. I looked at The Keeper and a tear of achievement welled up in my eyes and down onto my drying netherwear. 500 miles were ours, done and dusted.

DAY 27

Date: Friday 27 July

Start: 04:55 at Bar-sur-Aube

Finish: 13:55 at Châteauvillain

Distance: 39.2km (24.5 miles)

Total: 844km (528 miles)

Daily average: 31.3km (19.5 miles)

When the alarm rang, I did not want to listen. I was tired; it was too early; and I desperately wanted more sleep. The Keeper nudged me gently, sensing my fatigue, and sweetly handed me a cup of tea. I knew I had to get up and make use of the cooler hours; I was going to find it hard if I did not. But just then, actioning those sensible thoughts was another matter. The Keeper nudged me again, and I reluctantly rose to my feet.

We had left the town behind us and were walking through fields of vines as the sun rose. We watched in awe once more as the golden light spread its wings across the vines and turned the land from a state of rest to one of promise.

As the vines came to an end, the fields started to open before us, and there, in the middle of a cut hayfield, was a wild boar. He was having a fine old time rooting around for his breakfast and taking pleasure in the fresher air. On noticing us, he snuffled some more before leisurely trotting off for cover. He was a local, obviously, and as such fully up to speed with the future dates of the hunting season.

A couple of hours later, coming down out of some woods and into a valley, we were brought up short by a tall and ancient-looking tiled wall. We followed the wall for some time until we found ourselves at the gates of Clairvaux Abbey. Once a successful

Cistercian order founded in 1115 by St Bernard, the original building is now in ruins. However, the very appealing replacement building of 1708 is still there, as is a jail. France's No. 1 high-security jail to be precise, which partially occupies the grounds. Forbidding watchtowers and 20th century jail cell blocks make for an interesting juxtaposition to the calm of the monastic buildings.

Although open for tours (the abbey, that is, not the jail), we chose not to stay. We still had a long way to go to reach the town of Châteauvillain. Our guidebook's rounding down errors and omissions meant that the published route of 19 miles was going to be nearer to 23 miles.

We got back on the road, but with the afternoon came the heat, thirty-six degrees of tarmac-melting heat that melted us too. The air was so hot and heavy that we almost had to push our way through it, it was exhausting. We found ourselves in the middle of nowhere, drinking our water supply too quickly.

Looking at the guidebook, The Keeper reassuringly told me that 'the next village has a tap'. "How far is the tap?" I asked, desperately wanting it to be around the next bend.

"Not far," he replied carefully, adding, "I know you can do it."

With my head down under the baking sun, 'got to get to the tap, got to get to the tap' became my mantra and all I could think about for the next thirty-five long minutes.

With the village coming into sight, The Keeper suddenly turned left and into the local cemetery. *Hang on there, I am not that bad* I thought to myself, *there is still some life in the old wife*. Then I realised, of course, the tap of our dreams was the tap for watering the graveside flowers.

Not caring in the least where the water came from, I followed The Keeper into the cemetery. We found the flower care corner and we found the tap. Collapsing with relief onto a stone bench, we turned our attention to cooling ourselves down.

I soaked a handkerchief and dabbed it about my neck and arms. The Keeper put his head down and emptied a bucket over it.

Revived, but with lank, dishevelled hair and water dripping off his well-developed nose, Bucket Head put his arms out and started stomping around like Frankenstein with flu. Just then, I heard the wrought iron gates of the cemetery creak open and I looked up. A beautiful young woman was dismounting from her bike.

She was obviously looking for a quiet moment amongst the well-behaved residents of the establishment. She was not looking for a pair of live oldies cavorting with a tap and a bucket. I stopped short, Bucket Head, his eyes and ears still full of water, bumping into me before realising we had an audience.

The young woman raised an amused eyebrow and summed up the situation with the forgiving single comment, "Chaud, n'est-ce pas?"

We tried to exit discreetly, to give the young woman her space, but it was not an easy task for a dripping Frankenstein and his amused bride.

The last six miles on the road were hot, very hot. The heat invaded me, and I wilted, to the point that I could barely drag myself into Châteauvillain. On the outskirts of the town, I fell into a heap. The Keeper, concerned, lifted my backpack onto his own shoulders and slowly talked me in. I needed liquid and glucose and I needed them quickly, so we headed for the first bar we saw. It was closed. The Keeper willed me to the second, but it too, was closed. There was a third up ahead. "Can you make it?" The Keeper asked. We got there, only to find that it was also closed. I could have cried, but I had no tears to shed. We inched on, eventually seeing an open ironmongery-cum-general store. On a bench in the shade, I drank two cans of coke and ate two chocolate bars without stopping for breath.

Twenty minutes later, driven by the high of my own 'sugar fuel injected' motor, I marched to our hotel.

DAY 28

Date: Saturday 28 July

Start: 08:05 at Châteauvillain

Finish: 12:05 in Arc-en-Barrois

Distance: 19.1km (11.9 miles)

Total: 863km (540 miles)

Daily average: 30.8km (19.3 miles)

Châteauvillain is a fortified town that has sat at a bend of the river Aujon almost since time began. It is a town that lives its history; its ancient houses made from local stone are occupied; and its monuments cared for as if they have only just come out of service.

A maze of tiny alleys, no wider than a shoulder's width, meander the town, connecting houses to watch towers, town gates, *lavoirs* and even a rotund dovecot capable of housing three thousand pigeons. But it is not on the tourist radar, and it is not wealthy. It is a fairy tale kingdom that lies waiting for a princely mayor with a marketing department to give it the kiss of a new life (and an injection of cash).

We left Châteauvillain by gently pushing open the large wooden door of its 14th century Porte Madame gate. We thought we would be leaving the fairy tale kingdom behind us but instead we had merely left the one that man inhabited and had entered the one the natural world did.

We were in the walled parkland and forest of the Parc-aux-Dames. From medieval times to the French Revolution, this had been the private hunting grounds of the château's owner and it had changed little. The traffic-free 672 acres are Châteauvillain's version of Richmond Park and magically, we had it all to ourselves.

We set off quietly, unable to disrupt the enchantment with idle chatter. Our silence was rewarded by the site of a large stag, complete with a full set of magnificent antlers. Side on to us, he was watching over his herd, his head raised, the monarch of his own glen. Catching our scent on the breeze he turned and silently disappeared into the trees. A fleeting vision that left us with a lasting memory.

With no more of the park to cross, we regretfully exited and spent the rest of our surprisingly pleasant morning amongst more trees. We were mainly on tracks used by forestry commission vehicles within the forest of Arc-en-Barrois. This 27,000-acre forest is one of France's largest and home to the village of its namesake, Arc-en-Barrois.

This village is on the tourist radar and its moderately sized centre obliged, offering a curated collection of boutique hotels and artisan shops. The one anomaly was the local chateau that sat, surprisingly, right in its heart, dwarfing the buildings around it. Since the Middle Ages, the château has been used chiefly as a hunting lodge by princes, royalty and French nobility. Now, however, the building is a fifty-room condominium, the occupants of which, I hope, patronise the village. Our excellent lunch, in a Michelin recommended restaurant, is perhaps evidence that they do.

Our home for the night was at a wonderful former hermitage. It was a special place with big views across the forest, excellent food and home to a barrel on legs, called 'Hastings'. That is the dog; the owner was the delightful Jean-Louis.

DAY 29

Date: Sunday 29 July

Start: 05:45 at Arc-en Barrois

Finish: 13:40 at Langres

Distance: 36.9km (23.1 miles)

Total: 900km (563 miles)

Daily average: 31.km (19.4 miles)

We crept downstairs at 05:20, hoping to find a sandwich left out for our breakfast. What we found instead was a laden breakfast table and a smiling Jean-Louis. A fellow hiker himself, he was going to give us a proper send-off, no matter what the time was. And what a send-off it was too, one that did not end at the breakfast table but at his garden gate. Jean-Louis stood with the gate open to the forest beyond, enthusiastically spinning his tea towel in the air, wishing us *bon randonné*.

A funny lot, us hikers. The night before, he had summed it up so succinctly: "When I am hiking, I am happy."

Twenty three happy miles later, after a journey that had taken us through fields, woodlands and a succession of quiet villages, we found ourselves at the base of a large limestone promontory. At the top of the promontory was Langres and where The Keeper had booked us a room.

Tired and thirsty, I looked up at the ancient town sitting high above me. "And just how am I going to get up there?" I questioned. I clearly needed help and I needed it fast.

I called an old friend, actually a few of them: Grace Jones, Aretha Franklin, David Bowie and Dolly Parton. That showed my age, it was disco time! My toes started tapping; my hips started swaying and, uncontrollably, my bottom added its signature wiggle. In this energised state, the backpack and I took off.

I was not a lone disco diva for long. On catching up, The Keeper diva joined in, banging his walking poles to the base beat and popping in his own addition of an odd hip shake.

Up we went, higher and higher, strutting our stuff like a couple of would-be John Travoltas on a travelator, until finally we collapsed, struggling for breath on a step just outside the city walls. Calling time on the evocation of our youth, we collected ourselves and walked back into our own middle age and Langres.

Langres, as well as being a washed rind cheese, is a fortified town that was built to be noticed. Known for its long ramparts, it still also has its seven fortified towers and seven gates. Its cathedral, with an 18th century facade that looked more suited to coal mining than worship, was rather disappointing, I thought.

In the evening, we caught up with Julie and James again and went out to dinner. Julie is a vegetarian, which in France means she is not of sound mind. The menu claimed to have a vegetarian option, but it was obviously hiding, as everything appeared to contain meat.

"I am a vegetarian. What, from your menu, can I eat?" asked Julie.

"You can have a salad," replied the waitress.

We all studied the menu, but each of the salads contained meat. Julie had a nice meal of lettuce and cheese. She has eaten a lot of lettuce and cheese in France.

At the end of the evening, we said fond farewells to our fellow travellers, as we would not be seeing them again. They had spent a few days following The Keeper's schedule and were not its greatest fans. They would be returning to their more leisurely approach and would arrive in Rome some weeks after us. I could not blame them.

DAY 30

Date: Monday 30 July

Start: 05:40 at Langres

Finish: 15:30 at Champlitte

Distance: 42.8km (26.8 miles)

Total: 943km (589 miles)

Daily average: 31.4km (19.6 miles)

As we tended to leave our hotel beds just after the other guests had found theirs, we became accustomed to settling our bill the night before. With this done, each early morning's exit routine was similar, but there was always a moment when something went awry, and this morning was no exception.

With politeness towards the slumbering guests, we quietly opened our bedroom door and gently closed it behind us. Then, stealthily descending the staircase as if we were absconding with the silverware and not just our backpacks, we came to the front door. The door, old and wooden with big metal bolts, creaked and groaned its annoyance at being handled so early. Patiently, we drew back each bolt, turned the large handle and slipped through.

The wrought iron gates across the courtyard were another matter. As we negotiated their various locks and levers, they would not be hushed or mollycoddled into quietness. We both tried, each whispering instruction to the other, until a set of whispered instructions from me was met with a set of whispered suggestions from The Keeper that had nothing to do with opening the gates at all. That shut me up.

Then it made me giggle, which I tried to hush, which made me giggle more, until my mirth gates were open even if the courtyard gates were not.

Hotel
Belvedere
Parking

With no alternative left, The Keeper pushed the screeching gates apart and me through them. Grabbing hold of my backpack as well as his, he marched us all to freedom.

Freedom was 26 miles of walking, a marathon distance. The route initially followed a quiet tarmac road to the village of Chilandrey. Here, we were reminded that it was a Monday and that rural France closes on a Monday. With no stores open, we took stock of our supplies and discovered (yet again) that they were limited: a boiled egg and a banana each, a few peanuts and a tube of Pringle-like crisps. We pressed on. We had no choice.

Walking along a particularly leafy section of a quiet road, each in our own little world, we were suddenly pulled up short at the sound of heavy beating on the earth. A second later, two adult deer came crashing through the undergrowth, passed in front of us and, in a heartbeat, were gone again. We stood stunned into immobility and silence, their bulk, smell and energy still with us on the path. Without consulting the other, we kept our ground and waited alert for other deer or the cause of the flight, but there was nothing more. We moved on, silent again, but this time not from politeness to our fellow man but in awe and admiration of our wild companions.

The Monday factor, together with the temperature and the day's distance meant that we had to occasionally ask for water. Two pelerins on the wrong side of fifty, with large smiles under floppy hats, were generally considered amusing rather than threatening. Our requests for water tended to be met with a friendly conversation and interest in our journey.

One such stop was at a building marked on our map as an ancient hospital. We knocked on what looked like the front door, which was opened a minute later by a small child who collected her mother, who collected her husband, who invited us in.

Inside was unexpected, unless a menagerie of parrots was what you were expecting. Parrots in their cages, parrots loose on the sofa, a parrot who jumped on the husband's shoulder.

I stood in flummoxed wonder but The Keeper, from the depths of some past school classroom, remembered the word *perroquet* and managed to keep the conversation flowing. The young family were charming - the children showed us their toys, and the parents offered us coffee. As we came to leave, we accepted our refilled water bottles with gratitude and discreetly pocketed the few vagrant sunflower seeds that came with them.

As this was our longest day of walking yet and we were doing it on extremely limited nutrition, my energy level waned and the last few miles were picked off very slowly. Thankfully, on the outskirts of Champlitte, we found a campsite that had a little bar for its happy campers and now happy visiting pelerins.

Reaching the bar, I fell onto a plastic chair in a stupor of thankfulness. As I was unable to move further, the barman brought his selection of cold drinks and sandwiches to my chair. Having made my choice, I then consumed them with indecent haste but such happiness that the bemused barman smiled his approval. Fully refuelled, we walked the last couple of miles to our hotel.

Dinner in the hotel that night was surprisingly good and pleasingly large. We sat outside on a small wooden terrace and ate whatever was given to us, almost as soon as it was given to us.

Replete, I sat back and thought about the day. We had set a goal and we had achieved it - that was something to celebrate. I was weary from a day of exercise but not tired of life, in fact I felt more alive than ever. I tingled with it. I looked across at The Keeper contentedly languishing in his chair. He looked happy. "Do you have a tingle?" I asked.

"No, sorry, we finished the crisps earlier," he replied.

DAY 31

Date: Tuesday 31 July

Start: 07:20 at Champlitte

Finish: 11:30 at Dampierre-sur-Salon

Distance: 21.0km (13.1 miles)

Total: 964km (603 miles)

Daily average: 31.1km (19.4 miles)

The afternoon before, as we had checked into the hotel, we were given a key for a room not in the main part of the hotel but in their tower. Dim-witted enough to not realise that the French might have the same view of hikers as the Brits, I dropped my guard. In favour of romance over scepticism, I naively accepted the key. "Let's go and see this intriguing room," I said with enthusiasm and set off.

Between roughly hewn stone walls and on flagstones worn down by generations of use, we made our way up an ancient circular staircase. Finding our door, I excitedly peeped in and was met with disappointment. The round room was surprisingly small and decidedly spartan. Opposite me was a window and, tightly squeezed in between the window and the door, a bed. Apart from a shower curtain and a whiff of gauze at the window, that was all the room contained.

We stepped directly from the door onto the bed and then The Keeper, stepping from the bed to the shower curtain, announced, "Look at this!" Suppressing a grin, he drew the curtain aside. Inside the space of a normal shower was a basin, a toilet and the shower. "Now that is efficient," he said. "I can attempt all three tasks at once." I fell back on the bed, hoping he did not. If it had not already happened, the nail in the romance coffin had been firmly hammered home.

This morning, leaving our circular cell, we went in search of breakfast and found it offered in an underground, windowless dining room. A further way, I assumed, of the hotelier's desire to impress their paying guests. Thank goodness we had sampled last night's meal, or we might have taken away a rather dim view of the hotel.

Back on the road, we had a very easy half-day of mainly country tracks through mixed farmland. We ended our journey at the door of a village château, somewhat earlier than we had expected. We rang the bell anyway, and a fine-featured willowy lady, wearing a beautiful smile and a pile of grey hair scooped up in a bun, opened the door.

She greeted us with such warmth and interest, skilfully getting past the fact that we were four hours earlier than her published arrival time, that we melted under her spell. Sitting us in her salon she drifted in and out, bringing tea in china cups, cakes on stands and pleasant conversation. Following our refreshments, we were shown to our bedroom, where flowers bloomed on the wallpaper, bedspread and curtains and fresh roses sat in vases. It was a delightful bouquet of a bedroom. Collapsing on the bed, I was just drifting off when I heard The Keeper quizzing me as he unpacked his backpack.

"Does she remind you of anyone, Goat? Remember reading to the kids? She reminds me of Madame from *Babar*, The Old Lady who is Babar's mother."

"We are in Celesteville and it is heavenly," I said in agreement as I fell asleep.

Whilst I slept, The Keeper, also known occasionally as Mr Duracell (whose batteries I wish I could remove sometimes), got busy with a thorough kit-washing exercise. Everything he owned that could be washed was scrubbed to within an inch of its life.

"Oh heck," I thought, waking from my nap and joining in the laundry mania. "How are we going to dry everything?" I pondered aloud.

We crept into the garden and found a fine old apple tree hidden away. Decorating its heavy boughs with our smalls, drying took no time at all. We returned to the château delightfully clean and trailing a hint of *eau de pomme* to add to the botanicals.

DAY 32

Date: Wednesday 1 August

Start: 05:45 at Dampierre-sur-Salon

Finish: 13:00 at Gy

Distance: 30.8km (19.3 miles)

Total: 995km (622 miles)

Daily average: 31.1km (19.4 miles)

Warm water from a plastic water bottle is not the most desirable of drinks. However, for most of the day, *l'eau chaude* was our only option. We did pass through some small villages hoping for a shop or cafe, but each time we were disappointed.

Out of necessity, we had to occasionally ask for water refills from obliging locals. Thankfully, however, we did not have to worry about our calorie intake. Babar's mother, Madame, had packed enough breakfast for a small herd of elephants, certainly enough to keep us two ellies going for the day. We were grateful for her generosity. It got us across the Saône river and kept us going on a disappointingly road-biased day.

Each day I looked forward to lunch, not only for the opportunity to eat but also for the opportunity to sit. From the moment we left one hotel to the moment we entered another, it was the only real chance I had to rest my body and take the weight off my feet. Some days I did not know which was more important, to eat or to sit. Depending on the day's mileage, our break could be anything from a quick five minutes to a leisurely thirty minutes. No matter how long it was, however, it was of great importance to me, and as such, care was exercised in choosing the right spot. The Keeper, I know, had sometimes dug deep into his patience reserves whilst we walked a frustrating mile or two before the right fallen log or bit of low wall was deemed acceptable.

Today, much to The Keeper's relief, with minimal fuss, we found an idyllic spot for lunch on the top of two huge round hay bales. The Keeper took a bit of a run and jumped up onto his, settled down and almost immediately started to tuck into his longed-for lunch.

I found that ascending the top of my haystack was a bit more challenging. I too took a bit of a run at it but just hit the side. Then I changed tack and tried to climb up, but it was tightly compacted and surprisingly smooth. I could not get a toe hold.

"Are you alright, Goat?" asked someone who was not doing a good job at hiding a smile behind his sandwich.

Climbing down from his rather superior position, The Keeper gave me a leg-up, followed by a shove-up and I too summited my hay mountain. Turning to thank The Keeper, it was my turn to hide a smile behind a sandwich. Seeking relief from his sweaty hat, he had honed his millinery skills and sat with a knotted handkerchief on his head. Not a good look, not a good look at all.

From our elevated positions, we both enjoyed a sumptuous lunch, which was just as well. When we arrived in Gy later that afternoon, we discovered that Wednesday was the town's half-day closing, including the restaurants. Dinner was a slice of takeaway pizza, bought from a van in the town square. At least I did not have to climb anything to get it.

DAY 33

Date: Thursday 2 August

Start: 05:40 at Gy

Finish: 14:00 at Besançon

Distance: 36.1km (22.6 miles)

Total: 1031km (644 miles)

Daily average: 31.2km (19.5 miles)

As we drew nearer to Besançon, the topography changed and sizable hills started to appear. Generally, we like hills, but the combination of today's hills with the high temperatures and the extended mileage was making us weary. As we slowly put away the miles under a relentless sun, we became obsessed with the need for a cold drink, any drink providing it came from a fridge.

Fridges, however, were absent today. As with much of our French walking, village after village had nothing to offer us but disappointment. We would walk into the centres hoping to find an open shop or a cafe and walk out again bereft, the unrequited need for a cold drink still raw in our dry throats.

We had been on our feet for six hours before we reached the fringes of Besançon's suburbia and found our chiller thriller. Sitting down in a roadside cafe, we asked for two large Coca Colas each 'as fast as possible please'. A sweet young slip of a waitress brought them straight to us, her eyes large and round with enquiry. Backpackers, particularly old British ones wafting an air of desperation, were intriguing.

Explaining our walk to her, the waitress asked with genuine concern if we were sure we wanted to do it. I looked at The Keeper and raised an eyebrow in question. Were we sure we wanted to do it? At that precise moment, with my boots off and dribbling coke down my chin, I looked better destined for incontinence than Rome. Then I saw in The Keeper's face both his answer and all that I felt reflected back at me. This was our adventure and ours to do together. It was liberating, strengthening and rewarding. The challenge had its testing moments, for sure, but there were also numerous highs and celebrations along the way. And aside from that, we were stocking up on shared memories to bore our future grandchildren with. Could there be a better way to spend eleven weeks?

Luckily for the waitress, our linguistic limitations protected her from the full vocalisation of this hiking tome. Instead, we nodded our heads and reassured her that, yes, we really wanted to do this.

With our thirst finally sated and water bottles replenished with ice-cold water, we left the cafe hand in hand. We felt capable, at least for a mile or two, of taking on the world, not just walking to Rome.

Refuelled and rehydrated, we negotiated the surprisingly large urban sprawl of our destination city and arrived at the Besançon hotel in good spirits. We were just receiving the 'fast track booking-in' service that we have become accustomed to, when the door of the hotel opened.

Two other hikers, accompanied by the gentle scent of 'fresh from the tumble dryer' stood beaming at us. Friends Penny and Phil had arrived with small backpacks and large smiles. I did a joyful jiggle but, mindful of mingling our differing scents, The Keeper and I kept the hugs brief.

Later, as we searched for supper, we were charmed instantly by the historic centre of Besançon. The city is folded into the bend of the river Doubs and contains an eclectic mix of architecture, buildings that have gathered over the centuries of the city's strategic importance. Capping the city is a dramatic 17th century citadel and as a backdrop are the Jura mountains, which we were going over next.

DAY 34

Date: Friday 3 August

Start: 05:30 at Besançon

Finish: 14:30 at Ornans

Distance: 35.9km (22.4 miles)

Total: 1067km (667 miles)

Daily average: 31.4km (19.6 miles)

With Penny and Phil gamely prepared for a pre-dawn start, we walked out of Besançon under the glow of its streetlamps. The Keeper of the Maps naturally assumed command and led from the front. Together, Penny, Phil and I jostled around at the back as mere foot soldiers following orders.

The day broke as we arrived at the monument of Our Lady of Liberation, dedicated to those of the city who had died in WWII. Our Lady is sited 200m above Besançon and offers a fine reward to those who climb to her. We stood and gawped at the vast, uninterrupted view. We could see both where The Keeper and I had come from and the Jura mountains where we were headed. To walk from one place to another is satisfying, but to be able to see, in panorama, your 'epic feat on feet' is another thing altogether. The Keeper drew me in for a quick hug, a quick whispered moment of 'I'm proud of you' and then we were away.

From there, we were in open countryside and, in a landscape that was developing a decidedly alpine feel, we had a rather nice day bobbling along.

Penny and Phil had carefully selected and booked onto one of the short-day excursions offered by the Keeper's Hiking and Travel service. So, after 13 miles and with the day supposedly drawing to a close, we all stopped for a cheeky beer. We were in a shady ravine at a fish-for-trout spot. Shallow pools had been stocked with fish and children were gaily playing lucky dip with rods and buckets.

The Keeper, in a relaxed, almost holiday mode, consulted his phone and confidently announced we were only 3 miles away from Ornans, which was 'just up and over the col of yonder ridge'.

Picking up the vibes of our leader, we casually finished our beers, took up formation and headed for the pass. Then The Keeper's phone, in fact all our phones, lost service. This was not good, especially as we did not have a paper map for the area. Carrying on in the direction we had been going we arrived at a T-junction and a signpost. To our right was a safe but longer road around the hills, and to the left was the uncertain but teasing possibility of a short trip up a valley and over the promised yonder ridge. We decided to turn left. After twenty-five hot minutes without a hint of a track or trail, we realised we had made the wrong decision.

Penny, kindness personified, searched around for something to lighten the mood. "But it is a lovely valley," she said, "and look, the cows have bells." And she was right; it certainly was a lovely valley. Its fields were green and lush and in the middle of them, with a pointed steeple and arched windows, stood a chocolate box of a church, white against a deep blue sky. Around the church, a scattering of decorative cows grazed contentedly, dulcet tones rising from the bells around their necks. Lovely, but we were not sure we wanted to see it twice, which in the end was exactly what we did. We regrouped and wearily retraced our steps in the furnace heat and started to walk the long way home.

Arriving some hours and many unscheduled miles later at our hotel, those cows and their bells were not enough to convince Penny and Phil to do it all over again the next day.

They reduced their two-day experience to a one-day taster and, nursing their sore feet, served polite notice on the Hiking and Travel company.

Venturing out to dinner that evening, we realised why Ornans was nicknamed the 'Little Venice of the Franche-Comte'. It was a town full of beautiful old houses, many of which were built on sticks along the banks of the river Loue. Looking into the water from the Grand Pont, I saw the town reflected in such a perfect image that it felt as if I had been absorbed into a jigsaw. At any moment, I expected the scene to break into a hundred pieces.

Mindful of the long day and the need for dinner before we all broke into a hundred pieces ourselves, we headed into a restaurant. At the table with French-speaking Penny, The Keeper had the following conversation:

Waitress, in her impeccable French: "*C'est tout?*"

The Keeper in his schoolboy everyone-can-understand-me French: "*Une carafe d'eau, aussi.*"

Waitress in her impeccable English: "I am sorry; I do not understand. I do not speak English."

Penny, with her impeccable French and impeccable manners, stayed mute, but there was a little hint of amusement as The Keeper gave up and asked, "Could we have a jug of water as well please?"

ENGLISH CHANNEL
HOME
Canterbury
Dover
Calais
Thérouanne
Arras
Péronne
Laon
Reims
Châlons-en-Champagne
Brienne-le-Château
Bar-Sur-Aube
Langres
Champlitte
Besançon
WE ARE HERE
Lausanne
Montreux
Col du Grand-Saint-Bernard
Aosta
Ivrea
Pavia
Piacenza
Fidenza
Fornovo di Taro
Berceto
Pontermoli
Cucca
San Gimignano
Siena
Bolsena
ROMA
BAY OF BISCAY
ADRIATIC SEA
TYRRHENIAN SEA
N
S
E
W

DAY 35

Date: Saturday 4 August

Start: 05:30 at Ornans

Finish: 15:10 at Pontarlier

Distance: 37.4km (23.4 miles)

Total: 1104km (690 miles)

Daily average: 31.6km (19.7 miles)

Although they were not going to join us walking, Penny and Phil offered to drive our backpacks on for us. The Keeper, who had grown Fagan-like in protection of his worldly goods, chose to keep his pack. I was not so protective. A day's amnesty for my back was too valuable to be missed, and I gratefully handed my pack to Phil.

Although it was a backpack-free day, it was also to be an exhausting one, the accumulation of the last thirty-four days finally catching up with me. I was tired, weary, fatigued, done in. Admirably (but perhaps a smidgen annoyingly), Mr Keeper-Bucket-Head-Duracell was still equipped with a full set of batteries.

With miles to be walked, we once again headed out in the dark and followed a river upstream. As we passed by a sleeping campsite, I could hear the rhythmical, soporific sounds of deep breathing and gentle snores emanating from the tents. It was nearly too much. I too wanted to curl up in one of the tents, anyone's tent, and sleep. Knowing this was probably not socially acceptable (or something The Keeper would get on board with), I kept my yearning to myself and kept going. We walked steadily on up the river valley, and as we did, the scenery changed from gentle woodland to farmland and finally to a dramatic gorge.

As the sun rose, so did our hunger. To keep me going, The Keeper had been feeding me chunks of banana, but I needed something more. Then, as if sent down from heaven, we detected the scent of freshly baked bread in the air, and at 06:55 we were the first, grateful customers of the *boulangerie* in Vuillafans.

With bags of croissants, bread and pastries, we headed for the hills and ate our breakfast amongst rows of vines. The sun was just beginning to heat the land and threw a warm and welcoming light across the leaves and grapes around us. The vineyard felt protective and inviting. I wanted to stay with those vines and, like some giant dormouse, curl up beneath them and sleep.

On our feet again, we continued climbing. We had a wall of mountains on our left and an ever-deepening ravine on our right. We could see right down the valley and would stop regularly to take in views of breathtaking magnitude.

We climbed higher still, and the geography changed once more, opening onto a vast plateau with sections of woodlands and lush plains. I so wanted to lie down on those plains, to make a mattress of the deep grass and sleep.

We headed on. The Keeper, practising a bit of psychology, set regular short targets. By not revealing the day's true mileage (which would have led to tears from me), he changed from feeding me bananas to feeding me a series of achievable goals. Focusing on these goals, I just put one foot in front of the other. There was not enough energy for anything else. I was fragile; I was monosyllabic; I needed to be handled with care.

Eventually, we reached the outskirts of Pontarlier, and there on a bench were Penny and Phil with smiles to lift the heart. Better still, they were waiting beside a handy cemetery; we were now flower tap aficionados, and we drank copiously to quench our thirst.

With my goal for the day near at hand, and fully hydrated from the '*eau du cimetière*', I perked up considerably. Together with Penny and Phil, we started to walk to our hotel. As we passed a house, a kind lady working in her garden asked if we would like a drink. The Keeper's vampire response tickled us and confused her. "Thank you, madame, but we have already drunk at the cemetery."

On reaching our hotel, and only then, The Keeper declared we had walked twenty-three miles. Grateful that the day had finally come to an end, I stumbled into our room, showered and, like the dormouse I had longed to be all day, curled up and slept.

Dinner that night was celebratory. I had overcome a difficult day and been rewarded with a wonderful nap; we had good friends to share it with (the dinner not the nap); and there was a promise of cooler weather on the way. What more could I want? I realised, at that very moment, it was not a lot. I also realised that a few weeks ago, the probability of finding joy and happiness in a low-budget, out-of-town hotel with a plasticised menu and homogenised lighting would have been low. The multiple layers of life would have got in the way and confused the simplicity of what really constitutes a good life. Tonight, I had been reminded.

DAY 36

Date: Sunday 5 August

Start: 08:10 at Pontarlier

Finish: 14:10 at Sainte-Croix

Distance: 24.1km (15.1 miles)

Total: 1128km (705 miles)

Daily average: 31.3km (19.6 miles)

We were in the hotel with Penny and Phil, making the best of an automated breakfast, when in bustled Chumley, who we had last seen on Day Two. Choosing not to fly for admiral reasons, Chumley had experienced electrical faults and a dubious cassock-wearing clergyman on her complex train journey to reach us. Despite all that, she was beaming, khaki-clad and ready to go. What a trooper.

Penny and Phil saw us off from the car park and, with Chumley by our side, we began another day, heading for the centre of town.

Pontarlier is known for absinthe, which it had produced profitably until its ban in 1915. Searching for an alternative revenue, the distilleries had switched to producing a pastiche, or, as we know it, 'pastis'. Our route took us past a number of these distilleries and well-known brands as we walked through the town and out into the countryside beyond.

Almost immediately after leaving Pontarlier, we started to climb, and as we did, so the architecture became more alpine and the temperature began to drop. After stopping for a coffee in Les Fourgs, we crossed some fields, joined a road, rounded a bend and stopped short in amazement. There in front of us was Switzerland. With that sudden realisation, as if being caught by a wave at the beach, a gush of excitement, achievement and relief hit us full-on. We had walked across France.

From sheer joy, my bottom commenced its signature wiggle, a move The Keeper now knew to be synonymous with happiness and not a bee in my pants.

Unconcerned therefore with my antics, The Keeper and Chumley swapped celebratory grins and map references.

We walked on through border control with our passports at the ready, hoping to be stopped, to be given an opportunity to express to someone, anyone, our achievement. We have walked here! But the border police no more than nodded their assent. Clearly, three hikers were not a threat to national security, even if one of them, possibly, had something in her pants.

We headed off across the fields to L'Auberson, passing hibernating ski lifts waiting for winter to awaken them. It was another world, lush and green and verdant. Gone were the arid fields and the unbearable temperatures. We had arrived in cheese and chocolate-making bovine utopia.

It was just after 14:00 when we reached our Swiss hotel. An upright, white-walled building bedecked with rows of blue, shuttered windows and flower boxes under a red roof, it was a perfect slice of vernacular architecture. We had had a shorter day, for which I was grateful. I needed time to catch my breath. In a slothful mode, I spent the afternoon going no further than the garden terrace, our room and the dining room.

The Keeper, still oozing wonder (at having reached Switzerland) and energy, tried my slothfulness but found it wanting. Instead, thankfully, he ventured off by himself exploring the part of Switzerland he now found himself in.

DAY 37

Date: Monday 6 August

Start: 08:00 at Sainte-Croix

Finish: 12:40 at Orbe

Distance: 23.0km (14.4 miles)

Total: 1151km (720 miles)

Daily average: 31.1km (19.4 miles)

A beautiful morning greeted us, which was just as well as it took the edge off the inflated Swiss prices that also greeted us at the hotel desk.

With a shorter day and cooler temperatures ahead, we stayed and enjoyed a leisurely, nutritious breakfast. This, and the fact that I had slept the best part of ten hours, finally gave me the upper hand on my earlier weariness. I was ready for business. Meeting Chumley outside our hotel, we headed off for the day. Chumley had also joined us a few years earlier in the USA when we had been hiking the Appalachian Trail. We reminisced how good she had been at spotting bears.

As there are no bears in Switzerland, apart from chocolate ones, Chumley turned her attention to looking for Via Francigena signs. Thanks to her observational skills and her keen cartography interests, she was promoted to the special position of Keeper's Assistant. I did not seek the lofty heights of promotion, which was just as well, as I was not offered one and remained bumbling around at the back.

Walking away from the centre of Sainte-Croix, its tourists and music box museum, we found ourselves in the other Switzerland, the one the Swiss keep for themselves. Green velvet hills, meadows stocked with wildflowers and long, long views that roll on until they meet the sky.

We continued to walk through, and enjoy, the agreeable plateau of Sainte-Croix until mid-morning, when our path took a steep turn downwards. We needed to descend through the Gorges de Covatannaz to reach the Schweizer Mittelland, a drop of 500m.

The river Arnon is responsible for making the gorge, cutting into the landscape as it flows downhill. When it is heavy with water, it bursts along, leaving rapids, heavy falls and clamour in its wake.

For us, in a dry summer, the Arnon was more playful. It sploshed and pooled its way downhill, occasionally spraying a fine mist of its water on our skin or tempting us with ponds large enough to swim in.

Cooled and humidified by the river's water, the gorge was thick with flora. Trees grown tall in search of light threw a dappled shade and ferns crowded around at their feet. It was an oasis of enchantment.

When we reached the bottom and had the gorge behind us, so too were the Jura mountains. Ahead on the horizon now were the formidable Alps; somewhere beyond them was Rome.

We spent the afternoon walking through vineyards, across fields and negotiating the odd railway line. Arriving in Orbe later that afternoon was like walking onto a pageant-ready film set. The entire old town of Orbe is part of the Inventory of Swiss Heritage Sites, which basically means it is ancient and beautiful. Huge baronial-style flags hung off the buildings in the main square and riotous colours from facades, shutters, flower boxes, even flowerpots, were everywhere.

DAY 38

Date: Tuesday 7 August

Start: 05:30 at Orbe

Finish: 14:45 at Lausanne

Distance: 38.4km (24.0 miles)

Total: 1190km (744 miles)

Daily average: 31.3km (19.6 miles)

The Keeper and his new assistant were having a fine old time, cross-referencing maps and successfully charting shortcuts to the day's journey.

But confidence can sometimes lead to misjudgement. We were about to find that out.

Half a mile down a woodland track, at the end of the morning's third 'short cut', we came to a dead end. We had nowhere else to go but back the way we had come or up a seemingly impenetrable embankment. I thought we should take a breather and democratically decide what to do. The Keeper, an autonomous fellow, took stock and shot into the undergrowth.

After climbing through brambles, scrambling over felled trees and crawling along, head down and bottom up, he called down to reassure us that it was 'just fine'.

Chumley and I looked at each other in disbelief. Of course, it was not 'just fine', stupid man. Did he need reminding that Chumley and I were not spring chickens but chickens whose springs were beginning to droop? But what could we do? He was halfway up, and we were not. So off we went, falling over tree trunks, searching for foot holes in ivy, getting stuck on thorns, finding ants in unimaginable places.

When we reached the top, we emerged scratched, scraped and bitten but triumphant, with a childish sense of glee clipping at our heels. A glee that lasted for about two minutes before we found our voices and insisted on only following the designated path. Even though we had taken on and beaten our own 'Tough Mudder', Chumley and I knew we did not want to do another.

Later that morning, my brother rang me with the awful news that my father had just passed away. We walked into Lausanne with heavy hearts. Leaving Chumley and The Keeper, I made a sad and unscheduled return to the UK.

On my way home, I wrote to all those friends and family who had been following my blog. I was deeply touched and moved by the number of kind responses I received.

> *A quick note to let you know we are well, but there will be a slight pause with the updates. Sadly, on Tuesday, 7 August, my father passed away. He was nearly eighty-nine and suffering from dementia, so it was not entirely unexpected.*
>
> *When the Keeper and I walked the Appalachian Trail in 2013, my father had loved receiving those updates. He would also call us regularly and his enthusiasm, humour and interest were hugely encouraging.*
>
> *So, I will be continuing my updates in a few days, and I look forward to writing them. And I will have him, his love and his interest in mind as I do so.*

DAY 39, 40 & 41

Date: 8, 9, 10 August

Start: 05:30 at Lausanne

Finish: 14:00 at Montreux

Distance: 98.8km (61.8 miles)

Total: 1289km (805 miles)

Daily average: 31.4km (19.6 miles)

Chumley and The Keeper walked eastwards around Lac Léman. As they only had to keep the lake on their right, they didn't get into too much trouble. I joined them again in Martigny.

DAY 42

Date: Saturday 11 August

Start: 07:45 at Martigny

Finish: 15:15 at Orsières

Distance: 27.0km (16.9 miles)

Total: 1316km (822 miles)

Daily average: 31.3km (19.6 miles)

As I had arrived late the night before, a 07:30 start and a hearty hotel breakfast were agreed. The 07:30 start was achieved but the breakfast, thanks to a large party of people on the mature side of life (whose nationality will remain anonymous, *jawohl*) was more challenging. The coffee machine was hogged by 'double dosers' and the brown bread did not have time to nestle on its board before it was set upon and devoured. It was feral courtesy. We stalked the buffet for anything we could come by and tucked a consolation boiled egg into our packs.

Since the Romans, Martigny has held the strategically important position as protector of the pass over the Alps, now known as the Great St Bernard Pass. Consequently, the town is littered with Roman remains. On our path alone, we passed the footings of a large villa (incongruously on display underneath a multi-storey car park), a temple and thermal baths.

Leaving the town, we started to ascend as we too, following in the steps of the Roman traders, were about to begin our journey over the Alps.

After a few hours, we stopped at a pretty hamlet and had a coffee outside a wooden chalet restaurant. Sitting there, happy to be free of our backpacks and caught in the mellow of the moment, The Keeper shared with us his thought for the day.

ENGLISH CHANNEL
HOME
Canterbury
Dover
Calais
Thérouanne
Arras
Péronne
Laon
Reims
Châlons-en-Champagne
Brienne-le-Château
Bar-Sur-Aube
Langres
Champlitte
Besançon
Lausanne
Montreux
Col du Grand-Saint-Bernard
Aosta
Ivrea
Pavia
Piacenza
Fidenza
Fornovo di Taro
Berceto
Pontremoli
Lucca
San Gimignano
Siena
Bolsena
ROMA
WE ARE HERE
BAY OF BISCAY
ADRIATIC SEA
TYRRHENIAN SEA
N
S
W
E

"It is always reassuring to have a boiled egg about your person."

Out of innate politeness, we agreed. These ready-wrapped pops of nutrition were indeed valuable assets. After a minute, we also agreed that if discussing the merits of boiled eggs was all that we were capable of halfway up a beautiful mountain in Switzerland, then euthanasia was merited.

We walked on, up and up until the village of Sembrancher and a restaurant's very appealing *menu du jour* took our eye. Sod the boiled eggs.

Having enjoyed a delicious lunch, we left the restaurant and made our way along a narrow side street. Sitting beside the village water pump was a fellow hiker, a surprisingly rare sight. We were just passing the time of day, sharing the normal hiker-to-hiker information, when a car drove up and screeched to a halt beside us. Blocking the road with their car, four burly men got out.

Oh cripes, I thought, *are we in danger?* Hang on, they are wearing matching shirts. Are we about to be robbed by coordinating bandits? How Swiss.

In fact, we were being 'chanson bombed'. Yes, song bombed, with the blessing of the local tourist board. Having performed to us, twice, both times brilliantly, they got back in their car and drove off looking for other unsuspecting visitors to barbershop bomb.

Saying both amused and bemused goodbyes to our fellow hiker, we moved on and spent a very agreeable time climbing the Swiss countryside. We passed through mountain villages, across rivers and over lush pastureland. As we climbed, the mountains around us grew in stature until, at Orsières, we were surrounded by an imposing mass of them.

Arriving at our hotel, we got busy with the domestic duties, The Keeper kindly offering to hang out the washing whilst I had a nap.

A few hours later, I thought I would retrieve the washing from the balcony. Whoops, no

balcony. "Where's the washing?" I asked. The Keeper looked out of the window at a big tree in the middle of a patch of grass. It was decorated with our clothes.

"I'm not sure Orsières wants to view our underwear," I said, hurriedly putting on my boots to retrieve it.

"I'd wait a bit if I were you," replied The Keeper. I looked back at the tree. Someone was sitting against it, enjoying the big scenery from beneath our smalls.

DAY 43

Date: Sunday 12 August

Start: 07:30 at Orsières

Finish: 15:40 at Col du Grand St Bernard

Distance: 30.7km (19.2 miles)

Total: 1346km (841 miles)

Daily average: 31.3km (19.6 miles)

This was the big day, one of the days I had been most looking forward to and by far the most apprehensive about. It was the one day Chumley was really here for. The one day for which The Keeper had insisted we pack the extra weight in safety kit. We were ready, we had boiled eggs, and we were at the meeting point on time. But we did not have our chum. A couple of minutes later, she came hurrying along.

"Sorry, sorry," she said, "I couldn't get away as my hotelier wanted to kiss me."

The hotelier, by all accounts an affable man, had got carried away in wishing Chumley *bon courage* for the big day ahead of her. The unflappable Chumley had not been perturbed; she had simply quelled his exuberance by the deft positioning of her equipment against his. "Jolly useful, these walking poles," she commented whilst marching on. The Keeper raised an eyebrow and made a mental note to keep a closer, more protective eye on his regiment.

We were walking from Orsières to the col of the Great St Bernard Pass. The pass sits at 2473m, which is higher than Snowdon standing on top of Ben Nevis or about 2000 ft. higher than Mount Washington.

Orsières sits at 900m but because of the ups and downs of the route, we were going to

have to climb 2000m. Or if you speak in Fitbit, that is 670 flights of stairs. And so were our backpacks.

Well, if Napoleon and 44,000 soldiers could do it, so could we. So off we set. We climbed to Liddes along the bank of the river Dranse, then on to Bourg-Saint-Pierre. Conventional, sensible people call it a day here and do the remaining ascent the day after. But not The Keeper, and therefore not The Keeper's Assistant or his foot soldier.

Sharing a wistful look at the Bourg-Saint-Pierre hotel, Chumley and I moved on and followed The Keeper out of town.

We climbed higher again, until a steep zigzag track brought us out to the Barrage de Toules dam.

Finding a bench and a spectacular view, we had a quick boiled egg moment and then ventured off again. The number and variety of wild flowers and butterflies surprised us especially so after we had passed above the tree line. Meadows were salads of herbs, flowers and grasses. Rosebay willowherb was in abundance amongst the rocks and delicious wild raspberries were growing handily beside our tracks.

Walking through one treeless ravine we heard a reoccurring loud whistle: the warning call of the marmot. We could just see Mr Marmot standing meerkat-like on a stone, industriously calling out down the valley.

On and on we climbed until, surrounded by patches of snow, we looked up to a rocky outcrop and saw the promise of sanctuary: the roofline of the Saint Bernard Pass hostel. Never has the sight of a roof given me so much joy. Were we truly nearly there? Just below the outcrop, I could make out a person picking their way along a path, accompanied by three St Bernard dogs. Yes, we were nearly there.

Finally reaching the pass itself, we sat down gratefully on the terrace of a bar and enjoyed a celebratory beer. With the hard work over, a sense of euphoria (from what we had achieved, not from the beer) passed through each of us. We had asked for demanding and constant work from our bodies and they had responded, rewarding us at the end with a release of endorphins that were now fizzing inside of us. Involuntarily, the corners of our mouths kept curving upwards; unable and unwilling to stop them, we sat grinning inanely at each other.

With the afternoon drawing in, the last of the day trippers were making ready to go. We watched them climb into their soft seated cars or onto their air-conditioned buses without jealousy. We too could have chosen to travel to the pass by car. To speed up the mountain road, take in the view and the trinkets and speed away again, on towards the next destination. But that would have meant forsaking our journey, forsaking the very real sense of delight in being here in favour of the arbitrary need to be there.

We were staying at the hotel of the Hospice du Grand Saint-Bernard. The hospice was founded by Saint Bernard de Menthon in 1050 to accommodate pilgrims and travellers. It has been in continuous use for nearly a thousand years and has never closed its doors in all that time.

Having finished our beers and with the temperature plummeting, we walked up to those doors to gain our entrance. The outside of the building is plain, built and decorated, because of its position, to withstand all the weather that gets thrown at it. But inside, it is a different story; there is a sense of peace and devotion; religious art and icons hang on its white walls, and an ancient, gilded chapel sits in deep protection within its vaults.

My endorphin moment gave way to an overpowering sense of the past and to the now familiar sensation of walking in the footsteps of those who had gone before. Like us, thousands of travellers had sought sanctuary here, had opened the door of the hospice and found warmth, food and a place to rest. Could a building absorb emotion? Could it resonate with a thousand years of gratitude? Or, more likely, was I simply suffering from the altitude and beer. I put my musings aside and went off to find our room.

Later, lying in a soft bed between clean sheets, a deep feeling of safety and contentment came over me. As I drifted towards sleep, I again felt the presence of long past guests, and in their ethereal care and comfort, I slept.

DAY 44

Date: Monday 13 August

Start: 08:15 at Col du Grand St Bernard

Finish: 17:15 at Aosta

Distance: 30.0km (18.8 miles)

Total: 1376km (860 miles)

Daily average: 31.3km (19.5 miles)

We awoke in cloud and began our day with limited visibility and a long way to go. We were heading for Aosta, and to get there we had the major descent of 1890m (6201ft) to consider.

Wearing our extra clothing and rain jackets, we stepped out in excited anticipation. Beside the hostel was a small lake and, through the heavy mist, we could just see the first of the morning light playing on the water. Around the lake's edge was the path we needed to follow.

Our first target was to find Italy and we managed to tick that off two minutes later by bumping into the border signpost. We paused in the simple wonder of what the sign meant: we had walked across Switzerland. Not only that, but we had also put away the UK, completed France and were about to enter the country of our destination. The Keeper and I hung off the signpost in celebration whilst Chumley, the only witness to our delight, recorded the moment on her phone.

We were now in the Italian Valle d'Aosta, and the mist was giving way to rain, which made the going underfoot a bit more challenging. Slowly, we picked our way across the mountainside, down to the village of Bourg-Saint-Rhémy and a well-timed (and much better, Italian priced) coffee. With the coffee over, and the rain abating, it was out again

Italie
I

to put some more downhill miles behind us. A few hours later, and at 1264m, we came to the wonderfully named village of Etroubles.

On 20 May 1800, having got through the pass himself, Napoleon stayed the night at this village. Given he also had 44,000 soldiers with him who demanded food and shelter, is it any wonder the village had experienced its troubles.

After a few more miles we came to the Ru Neuf, a 15km path that follows the course of a 14th century water channel.

The whole of the Aosta valley used to be irrigated from a very elaborate system of *rus* (water channels) that took water to even the smallest of fields. Many of the larger canals are still in use today and we walked beside these, following the path before heading into the town of Gignod (936m). We trundled further downwards again, finally arriving at Aosta nine hours after we had left the col.

Even though we knew Aosta was our destination, it had only meant a beer, a bath and a bed. For the entire day, we had given it no more thought than that, our energy, both mentally and physically, had been focused on our descent.

We were somewhat surprised, therefore, to find ourselves arriving at a metropolis, and one that needed navigating. Aosta is a bustling, busy, noisy tourist town at the junction of the major roads to France and Switzerland. As it sits at the confluence of two rivers and at the end of the Little, as well as the Great, Saint Bernard Pass, it has always been of strategic military importance. Ancient buildings, Roman walls, gates and bridges abound, as do the tourists eager to see them.

As we neared the centre, the density of the tourists increased. Gorgeous, narrow roads lined with ornate buildings were thick with them. A mass of international camera clickers intent on ticking off the 'must-see' places on their itinerary. And who could blame them? The problem was, they all wanted to do it at the same time.

We had come off the hills where our habitat for days had been a natural one in an expanse of green space. Here, we felt hemmed in, channelled by the throng of humanity. Unable to turn without knocking the ice cream from someone's cone, we fell into single file and walked straight to our hotel.

Chumley had skilfully arranged a walk that had gone right across one country and taken in two others. Sadly though, tonight was to be her last night with us. Having dug deep into our backpacks and come up trumps with clean clothes to match our cleaned bodies, we hit the town. Well, that is what we intended. In reality, standing at the hotel door, we decided we could not face the scrum and headed for the hotel bar instead.

Sipping a large cocktail in the safety of the hotel's plump upholstery, I felt cocooned and protected from the spatial needs of others. I raised my glass to the other two opposite me and contentedly, we swapped an introverted 'cheers'.

Then Mr and Mrs Insensitive came in and plonked themselves needlessly on chairs right next to mine. Whilst Mrs Insensitive studied travel guides, Mr Insensitive busied himself with electronics. Out came the phone, on went the earphones and on went a podcast. The trouble was, the podcast was so loud, I was included, whether I desired it or not, in its audience. And I did not particularly need or want a self-help guide to finding fulfilment and the meaning of life. I had just walked from Hampshire to Aosta; I felt fulfilled enough thank you very much. I wondered why he felt he needed it. They were obviously touring and had a beautiful city to explore, was that not enough? I thought about proposing to him that tonight he switched off the podcast and tomorrow he walked the hills around the city. That would sort him out.

Instead, my cocoon invaded; I opted for a simpler way out and motioned to the others that perhaps it was time to eat.

We enjoyed an exceptionally good meal and an even better bottle of Barolo in the hotel's restaurant. We also enjoyed the company of the head chef, who, with great gusto, positivity and humour, spent more time on our side of the kitchen door than his. I doubt whether he needed a self-help podcast (although perhaps his sous-chef wished for one occasionally).

DAY 45

Date: Tuesday 14 August

Start: 08:00 at Aosta

Finish: 16:10 at Chatillon

Distance: 30.4km (19.0 miles)

Total: 1407km (879 miles)

Daily average: 31.3km (19.5 miles)

We left Aosta as the city was readying itself for another day. Shop windows were being cleaned, awnings wound out and cafe chairs placed appealingly to catch the passers-by. Chumley walked with us as far as the Porta Praetoria city gate where, beneath walls that have stood since 25BC, we joined our farewells to the infinitesimal number that must have been said before us.

We began to make our way further down the Aosta Valley, walking from village to village as we did so. The villages cling precariously to their bit of mountainside, houses and churches juggled together on any piece of semi-flat land available. Our path would often take us directly in front of homes and their open windows. People would stop their lives (and sometimes their lunches) to greet us.

On one such occasion, we were walking through a tiny passageway, no wider than our shoulders, when someone called out, “Signora.” A gentleman, alerted by his friendly dog, was calling to me.

Marcello invited us in for coffee. Well, he invited me, but The Keeper, determined to not miss out, came in too. A benevolent man, Marcello was filling his days by recording data on all the Via Francigena hikers as they passed by. With an instant ease between us, born of his unguarded hospitality and our pleasure at receiving it, we sat together at his kitchen table and I wrote our details into his record book.

As we travelled between these homespun villages, astonishingly romantic castles appeared at every turn. Like architectural tiaras, they crowned almost every peak down the whole of the Aosta Valley. For the first few hours, we were wonderstruck by this fable-like land. By the afternoon, we were a little more castle-conditioned, but still intrigued enough to divert slightly and visit Castello di Fénis.

Known for its towers, battlement walls and position near a main road, Castello di Fénis is on the tourist trail. Arriving at the entrance booth from a little-used footpath and not from the car park, we found ourselves at the back of a group of visitors. It was like arriving late and incorrectly attired to a party. The guided group, who had chosen to observe their holidays from a safe and clean distance, turned and looked us up and down with a disdain. Hanging limply unsaid from the corners of downturned mouths was the question, *were the unwashed really going to accompany them on their tour of the castle?* We held our ground long enough to take some photos, exude our unique odour (hopefully), and then left them to it.

Later that afternoon, we arrived at the town of Chatillon and at the door of Guido and Anna, our B&B hosts for the night. A charming couple, they decided we were far too tired (which we were) to walk into town for supper. Guido would take us in his car, a Fiat Panda 4×4 that had more years under its camshaft than we had had boiled eggs. I climbed in the back and The Keeper folded himself into the front, his nose poking attractively through his knees.

Off we screeched, Guido's alter rally driver ego hitting the gas pedal. Having toured the back alleys of the mountain town (for either his pleasure or ours, I am not sure), he screeched to a halt depositing us outside our restaurant. We looked back to see a puff of smoke and the exhaust of the Panda as it disappeared up the street. Having eaten, he was there waiting for us and off we screeched again: The Panda Rally of Chatillon.

DAY 46

Date: Wednesday 15 August

Start: 08:05 at Chatillon

Finish: 15:05 at Verrès

Distance: 22.3km (13.9 miles)

Total: 1429km (893 miles)

Daily average: 31.1km (19.4 miles)

From our bedroom window that morning, we could see right across the Aosta valley. In sight, adorning the top of yet another rocky promontory, was the silhouette of the castle, Ussel. This castle was last owned by Herr Bich, the entrepreneur who bought and profited from Biro's patent. Repacking our backpacks for the fourty-sixth time and safely stowing our own Bic pen, we headed down to Anna and Guido's sunroom for breakfast.

Whilst Anna had cooked a hearty breakfast, Guido was anxious he too should play a part in the start of our day. Putting on his trainers, he walked us out to the Via Francigena path, chatting away, thankfully in French rather than Italian. After a hearty uphill climb, he turned for home, wishing us courage for our journey. As it was probably some years since he had seen his seventieth birthday, Guido was obviously as fit a hiking man as he was a fine rally driver.

We were walking on the south-facing side of the Aosta Valley. With plenty of sunshine and fresh water coming off the mountains, the slopes have long been green and productive. Our path regularly took us through ancient domestic orchards, the fruit trees gnarly with age, and beside well-tended vegetable plots.

Passing by one such plot, I again heard, "Signora." A woman working in her garden was asking me to wait. With a woven basket, she collected handfuls of tomatoes and peaches and gave them all to me. It was a simple and unexpected act of kindness, for which nothing was expected in return. I lifted the gift to my nose and the fresh scent of the sun-kissed fruit floated up, making me smile. "*Grazie, Signora*," I said. Our benefactor, her own face creasing with a smile nodded her acknowledgement of my thanks.

We ate the tomatoes and peaches as we walked along, their juice dripping down our chins. They tasted even better than they had smelt.

It was an extremely relaxed day of hiking, until that is, we reached the town of Verrès. Here, our hotel decided to do the dirty on us and play hide-and-seek. It hid, and we spent more time than we cared to, seeking.

"What is the matter with this town?" The Keeper asked later, as we found ourselves playing the same game but this time seeking an open restaurant. Close to despair with hunger, we found a sort of wine bar-cum-hang out for locals, not so much on trend as on its last legs. Realising they served aperitivo, the Italian version of wine and nibbles, we went in and ordered. Up came two generous glasses of wine and one small plate of prosciutto. This was not going to work, you cannot stoke a furnace with a powder puff.

The Keeper asked for another plate and up came a further small plate of ham, followed by more large glasses of wine. At this rate, we were going to be under the table before our stomachs had sniffed a calorie. We would have to try a different tactic.

The Keeper went inside and negotiated a separate fee for a large plate of mixed aperitivo. That worked. We waited in anticipation for our salami, hams, cheese, pickles, tomatoes and more. We received bread and cheese; something had got selectively lost in translation. At least the wine had stopped arriving and I would be able to walk, upright, back to the hotel.

With effort, we ate exactly what we had eaten for breakfast and for lunch and headed back. Choosing to walk a different route to the hotel, we passed by a garden lit with fairy lights and populated with linen draped tables. An appealing open restaurant. Neither of us commented.

DAY 47

Date: Thursday 16 August

Start: 08:00 at Verrès

Finish: 14:40 at Pont-Saint-Martin

Distance: 26.3km (16.4 miles)

Total: 1455km (910 miles)

Daily average: 31.0km (19.4 miles)

From Verrès, we walked along the valley bottom. As bottoms go, it is not a very wide one and shared with differing filaments of motion, the river Dora Baltea, a train line and two main roads. We wove between, over and sometimes under these for much of the morning before coming into the medieval village of Bard.

Bard, with its many 16th century buildings, is overlooked by Forte di Bard, set on a hilltop above. The village's first fortress dated from the 11th century but was razed to the ground by Napoleon's troops when he crashed through the valley in 1800. The present fort, built in 1838, has never seen battle and now houses a rather nice-looking hotel and opera space. Having neither the time nor the clothes to sample such niceties, we headed off towards Pont-Saint-Martin.

If we had approached Pont-Saint-Martin by car, we would have taken the SS26, driving along its smooth but characterless tarmac. However, we were lucky enough to approach it on foot, along an old Roman road. "Look at this," I said, pointing down at the stone flags. When Roman carts had made their journeys in and out of the town, their wheels had gradually worn two grooves, a cart width apart, into the flags. These grooves of history were now at our feet and, with wonder, we followed them into the town.

The town itself takes its name from a 1st century Roman bridge that, incredibly, is still in use. We went to see it and judged the best view to be from the well-positioned terrace of a nearby bar. This was lucky as they were serving much needed nutrients in salad form and we were too early to go on to our accommodation anyway.

Having killed an hour in the bar, we went off in search of a new form of lodging for us, an *apartment agricole*. Written instructions described the location as *within a farm, close to the town*. Lovely, we thought. Until we realised 'close' was written for wheels and not boots. And, oh dear, *apartment agricole* was more *agricole* than apartment. With two fingers, I gently lifted the corner of the bedding. An odour of past residents assaulted my nose and a 'we are not staying here' left my lips.

Tired, and by now nearing day's end, our options were few. I sat, dismay rendering me mute, whilst The Keeper did some research. Two miles away, there was a bed available. "Can you make it?" asked The Keeper. "It's our only choice," he added.

Could I really hobble two more miles? I had to. "OK, let's go," I responded.

We arrived at an old stone house and to a warm greeting by its lady owner. She showed us up an ancient set of stone steps and into an attic bedroom. It was a simple room, just a bed and a net at the window. Electricity was obviously a recent addition, borrowed from the nearby pole on the street and looped in through the window. The plumbing, by the look of it, was not so recent. The bathroom included an original hip bath and curiously, a hose. Whilst The Keeper distracted our hostess, I lifted the corner of the bedding. Not only was there beautiful linen, wonderfully clean, but it had been starched and pressed. Hallelujah, our bed for the night was sorted. Now, all I had to do was work out what to do with the hose.

DAY 48

Date: Friday 17 August

Start: 06:45 at Pont-Saint-Martin

Finish: 12:30 at Cascinette d'Ivrea

Distance: 23.5km (14.7 miles)

Total: 1479km (924 miles)

Daily average: 30.8km (19.3 miles)

With a smile for his early bird customers, the baker handed us croissants and pastries plucked straight from his ovens. Clutching them to us, their delicious aroma just escaping from the paper bag, we walked out of town until we found a seat in the early sunshine and ate with relish.

The day continued as agreeably as it had started. We travelled through a lush countryside, the scenery gradually changing from mountainous to hilly-rural as we progressed.

There were two recurring themes for the day: kiwis and goldfish, unsurprisingly not together.

Threading us through ancient stone villages, around domestic allotments and across farmland, the Via Francigena also took us directly under several long kiwi tunnels. Often, there was no other choice of route, the supporting pergolas had been built right over the path if that was the flattest land available to the farmer. The kiwi plants were in full health, their ripening fruit hanging down and knocking at our hats and shoulders as we passed through.

The goldfish we would see swimming in the village water troughs. Throughout our journey across Europe, most of the ancient villages would have an equally ancient water pump and stone trough. Many were still working and left as such; others, perhaps not working, were decorated with plants. Peculiar to this region of Piedmont, most troughs were embellished by the addition of these aquatic orange inhabitants.

Arriving in Ivrea, we had plenty of time for a leisurely lunch. Browsing through the guidebook, we continued the orange theme as Ivrea is apparently the home of 'The Battle of the Oranges'. Held in the days leading up to Lent, it involves thousands of townsfolk throwing (with some violence) four million oranges at each other. Interesting, if you have a burning desire to be beaten black and blue by orange squash missiles.

We spent the night in the tower of a contemporary hotel and under another set of perfectly clean sheets.

DAY 49

Date: Saturday 18 August

Start: 07:30 at Cascinette d'Ivrea

Finish: 15:45 at Santhià

Distance: 32.9km (20.6miles)

Total: 1512km (945 miles)

Daily average: 30.9km (19.3 miles)

This was a long day, during which we left the Aosta Valley and walked out onto the flats of Piedmont. The temperature was rising again, and shade was in short supply, especially in the latter part of the day which was mainly on hard, unforgiving roads.

At one point, desperate to sit in some shade, any shade, we hunkered down under a flyover. We sat with our backs to a concrete wall, in amongst dirt and debris, with just the metal crash barrier between us and the road. "Nice here, isn't it?" one of us needlessly remarked to the other.

By the time we were approaching Santhià, I had had enough of the sun beating down on me and the tarmac blazing it back. In fact, I had just had enough.

Then, through the haze of heat, I saw the answer to my dreams, my oasis in the desert of tarmac and dust: a Lidl supermarket. I picked up speed, surprising The Keeper who kept pace but just behind me, bewildered as to what I was up to but in a position of rescue if it was needed.

I opened the door to the supermarket but went no further than the down draft from the air conditioning. I stood there as the cooled air deliciously washed over my body and just grinned. "Come under," I said to The Keeper, as if I was offering some exquisite

Hawaiian waterfall. Soon, we were both grinning inanely but blocking the doorway.

"We will have to move," said the 6 ft. 4 in. voice of reason. But I was not ready to move, my head still carried the heat of the day. I wanted more.

Then I had an idea.

I walked over to a chest freezer, lifted the lid and put my head and arms in, as if I were looking for that last bag of frozen petit pois. With my backpack sandwiching me between the lid and the cold air, I had refound my waterfall, even if it was upside down.

"What are you doing now?" whispered The Keeper, as he sidled up beside me.

"Mm ooling off," I replied in a muffled voice from the depth of iceland.

"Well, you look ridiculous."

"I don't care. Ry it orsself," I suggested. So, he did but surreptitiously, as if no one would notice the bottom of an English hiker hanging out of a freezer.

"Bluffy farvellous," he conceded.

Sufficiently cooled and upright, we nodded our thanks to the bemused shoppers of Santhià and went to find our hotel. A very jolly hotelier, who booked us in with smiles and pleasantries, took us up to our room where he had a complete personality change. In a headmaster's voice, backed up by a stern listen-to-what-I-am-telling-you forefinger, he warned us not, for any reason, to open the windows. I thought he was going to add "Or you'll be caned."

As he left us, I stared quizzically at The Keeper. "What was that all about?" I mused.

And then it came to me: of course, we were in Santhià, and Santhià marks the start of mosquito country. We did not open the windows.

DAY 50

Date: Sunday 19 August

Start: 07:40 at Santhià

Finish: 14:40 at Vercelli

Distance: 28.8km (18.0 miles)

Total: 1541km (963 miles)

Daily average: 30.8km (19.3 miles)

The night before, when the hotelier had been in his jolly persona, he had confirmed that we could have breakfast at 07:00. However, at 07:05 it appeared we were the only ones who knew that.

We arrived at a darkened dining room, and it stayed that way, even when the outline of a plumply filled apron showed us to a table and grunted that we may sit but presumably not see or eat. So, we sat and twiddled our thumbs in polite anticipation.

At 07:15, we were given permission to see when the apron switched on the lights, illuminating an I-am-in-no-mood-today face. The Keeper and I looked at each other like naughty children unsure of our misdemeanour in the classroom.

Having passed her warning shot, the union member of breakfast ladies went back and forth from the kitchen to the buffet. For each journey, despite being equipped with two hands, just the one, single addition to the breakfast display was carried out.

Another couple of guests arrived and then one other. Each, in turn, was awarded a grunt and leave to sit but not to move. We had all been to school, so intuitively, we all obeyed and sat in expectant silence.

At 07:25, a further grunt announced the task, in its own time, had been completed and the breakfast buffet was open. The hotelier might have thought he had autocratic rule over his domain and its timetable but, clearly, the real power of the establishment was held in the strings of this apron unionist.

The Keeper and I helped ourselves to an unremarkable buffet.

Breakfasted, we made our way out of Santhià, protected by a layer of anti-mosquito spray, known more usually as Avon Skin So Soft. Earlier in this adventure, The Keeper had turned his not-so-small nose up at the proposition of applying a skin-softening product. I am sure he thought that, overnight, he would develop a peaches-and-cream complexion and breasts. But somewhere between Arras and Reims, he had been converted and now was mainly bite-free and, as far as I knew, had not developed a cleavage.

As we realised the night before, anti-mozzie cream was going to be a necessity. We were in the province of Vercelli and that meant we were about to enter the biting fields. Vercelli is the rice capital of Europe and as such, its land is one vast plain of paddy fields. These paddies are flooded in the summer by an intriguing and intricate water channel system. Less intriguing are the mosquitos that thrive in its stagnant water.

The Via Francigena guide gave us two options for this area: walking the paddy fields and facing the mozzies or walking the edge of a motorway and facing death. We chose the former. Hopping over the town's railway line to start our day, we bumped into two other *pellegrinos*, a rare but delightful occurrence. Catherine and Cameron were two Canadians walking from Lausanne to Rome. They had also decided on the safer option of facing the biting fields, so together we ventured out.

Usually, rice is double cropped, but some of the farmers were rotating rice with maize, so there were also masses of this tall plant. We were either walking on low banks over rice and water, the breeding grounds of our stinging enemy, or walking through tunnels of maize, the highways of our enemy. Either way, we were marked.

Temperatures were heading towards the mid-thirties, and there was little shade. Not that we would have been able to make use of shade anyway. Stopping, even slowing, meant you were prey and set upon by the bloodsucking enemy. The call of nature turned into the call of torture and was actioned in haste.

In this situation, we did the only thing we could do. We marched. For five and a half hours, we marched, and we swatted, and we sweated. Water and snacks were taken on the hoof and further layers of anti-mozzie cream were slapped on as we went. Thank goodness for the company of Catherine and Cameron, who added energy to the relentless pace and, together, our conversations got us all through.

Eventually, the town of Vercelli came into sight, and we spotted an out-of-town Carrefour with the promise of air conditioning and cold drinks. Behind the others, I dragged myself into the supermarket and fell onto the nearest chair in the cafeteria. I was spent. Even The Keeper admitted to feeling a 'little less than sprightly'. He did, however, have enough energy to request that I did not go in search of a 'petit pois' moment. Ha, I did not have enough energy to leave the chair, let alone walk the aisles of a hypermarket searching for a chest freezer. His dignity, by association, was safe.

Vercelli, in the plain of the river Po, is reported to be one of the oldest urban sites in Northern Italy, having been established in 600 BC. When we walked in, it was unsettlingly deserted for the August holidays. We did, however, manage to find one open restaurant, and over dinner, together with Catherine and Cameron, we nursed both our bites and another fine bottle or two of Barolo.

DAY 51

Date: Monday 20 August

Start: 07:30 at Vercelli

Finish: 16:30 at Mortara

Distance: 33.5km (20.9 miles)

Total: 1574km (984 miles)

Daily average: 30.9km (19.3 miles)

With the intrepid Canadian pacemakers by our sides, we once more marched, sweated and swatted. Covered in antihistamine cream to ease yesterday's mozzie bites, repellent to try and stop any future bites and sun protection, I became a giant oil slick on the move.

Paddy field after paddy field was put behind us. The monotony of the day was broken only by the welcome conversation between the four of us and the very occasional village to walk through. If we were lucky, the village would contain a water fountain or, if we were really lucky, an air-conditioned bar. We were really lucky only twice in the whole day.

A water fountain meant relief for the head, neck and shoulders. Like hens bobbing for seed, we would take it in turns to put our heads under the single spout and let the water run over us.

An air-conditioned bar meant all over sublime relief, cold air on our skin and cold drinks in our bodies. We entered with untold joy and exited reluctantly.

Eventually, tired and paddy-weary, we reached Mortara and went off to find our respective beds for the night.

The search for ours took us to a residential area on the edge of town and a very narrow street lined with houses on both sides. As we walked along the street, we ran a gauntlet of yard dogs that saw it as their duty to protect their domains. One by one, they barked (and occasionally snarled) at their gates as we passed by. When we finally stopped at the door of our B&B, the canine cacophony had not. There was no need for us to ring the bell.

The front door opened, and we were greeted by a softly spoken rotund gentleman who was obviously in possession of his hearing but perhaps a little sketchy on the whereabouts of his waist. He had positioned the elastic of his jersey shorts to sit just under his armpits, and the resulting effect further down the torso was a long way from appealing.

The gentleman invited us in and showed us through to a professor's enclave, a wonderfully eclectic room full of books, papers and music paraphernalia. Whilst booking us in, he told us he was a conductor/composer and that his daughter was studying music in Canterbury. I tried my best to concentrate, to be erudite and interested, but I just could not get beyond the shorts.

Clean, and needing to find dinner, we set the dogs off once more and ventured into town. A busy pizzeria enticed us in where, amongst an abundance of happy family groups, we consumed a large quantity of food and missed the company of our own family.

DAY 52

Date: Tuesday 21 August

Start: 07:50 at Mortara

Finish: 16:30 at Gropello Cairoli

Distance: 30.2km (18.9 miles)

Total: 1604km (1003 miles)

Daily average: 30.9km (19.3 miles)

Vincenzo, the musical waist-mislayer, and his wife Marie were good people who were slightly out of kilter with the rest of the B&B world. Our breakfast was a surprisingly intimate affair. Vincenzo, accompanied not only by his shorts but also his halitosis, sat extremely close to us and watched us eat, whilst Marie stood over us, also watching us eat.

Double scrutiny is a tricky start to any day. That, and the waft of halitosis and eggs, quite took our appetites away. The Keeper and I departed as soon as we were politely able.

Meeting up with Catherine and Cameron, who had stayed in a rather nice hotel (!), it was once more into the biting fields. And once more, we marched, sweated and swatted.

With a few hours behind us, we walked into the village of Tromello, where we were accosted. A man in a bright yellow T-shirt, riding a bike painted in the colours of the Italian flag, came straight at us. It turned out he was the local guardian of the Via Francigena (self-appointed or official, it was never clarified) and very proactive in his job. Feeling pleased with today's catch, he led us to a bar and generally bustled around, ensuring our well-being.

Charmed by the attention and good intentions of others, we were back on the road until we reached the town of Garlasco.

Profoundly grateful for their company and conversation over the previous few days, at Garlasco we parted company from our new Canadian friends. Catherine and Cameron had wisely decided to slow things down for a bit and intended to stay in town. The Keeper and I, not known for our sageness, were not slowing down. We went looking for our hotel and eventually found it another weary 7km on, at the edge of a motorway with a flashing neon sign announcing the 'Flower Hotel'. This did not look good.

We walked up to the desk, where the receptionist looked us up and down with an amused smile. She then suggested that we probably did not want a room by the hour. *Too right,* I thought. *Is the Pope Catholic? Does Dolly Parton sleep on her back? Look at us, of course we do not need a room by the hour.* Exhausted and itching from mosquito bites, the only thing protruding with interest, from either of us, were our water bottles.

The receptionist pointed to the other side of the U-shaped desk. Apparently, if we were interested in staying for the whole night, we needed to be on that side. We walked around whilst the receptionist rifled through a drawer of room keys. Finding the one she was looking for, she handed it over and nodded down the hall.

We opened our door onto a huge four-poster bed, draped unseductively in a hot pink polyester bedspread. At the end of the bed was a screen with an invitation to view free adult movies and 'have a nice time'.

The bathroom was monopolised by a circular jacuzzi bath big enough to swim in and contained another screen with another invitation to 'have a nice time'. Mirrors hung strategically or otherwise were everywhere.

Applying my now-usual room worthiness test, I lifted the corner of the bedspread. It was clean, and the sheets underneath were also clean. We were not clean and needed to be, and we were tired with no other options. We took the room and 'had a nice time' doing our laundry in the bath.

DAY 53

Date: Wednesday 22 August

Start: 05:45 at Gropello Cairoli

Finish: 09:30 at Pavia

Distance: 19.2km (12.0 miles)

Total: 1623km (1015 miles)

Daily average: 30.6km (19.1 miles)

Today we were going to journey further than our feet could carry us. We were returning to the UK for my father's funeral. Given this, we had to try and make up as many miles as we could both this side of the flight home and on our return.

Getting up early, we experienced our darkest start yet, our only illumination provided by the memorable neon sign of the 'Flower Hotel'. We were back in the biting fields, but thankfully it was the last stretch. It would have been a pleasant walk, watching the sunrise across the paddy fields, but the mosquitos robbed us of it. Under attack once again, we kept our heads down until we reached what we hoped would be the safety of the Ticino river. Here, the paddy fields stopped, and the Via Francigena followed the river into Pavia.

What could be nicer? A riverside path under the shade of riverside trees. Bliss. Or not. Unfortunately, those trees were laden with a nuisance that was new to us: The Furry Caterpillar. These tiny little darlings looked quite sweet and harmless but, if touched, they packed an urticaria punch which belied their size.

They thought it was the best game to drop on us and crawl around our necks, along our arms, across our shoulders and on our hats. Unknowingly, we even took a stow away or two back to the UK. Getting out of our walking kit that evening turned into a pass the parcel game, with a caterpillar prize within each layer.

We crossed over the river into Pavia on the Ponte Coperto, an attractive stone and brick arched construction built just after WWII in replacement of a 14th century predecessor. Pavia itself dates to pre-Roman times, and I would have liked to have investigated the city further. However, there was no time; we had a taxi waiting for us and a flight to the UK to catch.

We returned to Italy forty-eight hours later.

Arriving back, we got a wiggle on and put a few miles behind us before walking across the river Po into Piacenza to meet Catherine and Cameron for beers. Piacenza, a derivative of the words for 'pleasant abode', is just that, very pleasant indeed. Although it was heavily bombed in WWII, it still has several fine buildings. We met in Piazza Cavalli, the main square, and caught up with each other's news.

Earlier that day, Catherine and Cameron had been taken across the river Po by the self-appointed ferryman, Danilo Parisi, a famed character of the Via Francigena. Like other *pellegrinos*, they had been charmed by his hospitality and the formal signing of his *Book of Pilgrims*.

I would have dearly liked to have met Danilo and added our names to his record book. Here was a man who, in his retired life, not only spent his days helping people but who took the time to celebrate their chosen journeys with them. Reflecting on the events of our last few days and the realisation of the passage of time, I thought it summed up a positive life.

That evening, after a whirlwind couple of days of travel, emotion and focused walking, The Keeper decided a kit inspection was needed. Taking a good look at the inside of one of his water bottles, black slime was identified as a possible health risk. A vivid memory of us, the norovirus and a tent in Arizona came to my mind. I am sure neither of us wanted to go there again. From the determined way The Keeper placed his bottle on the counter, I gathered he had the same thoughts. The slime needed dealing with.

The conundrum, at 21:00 in a suburb of an Italian town, was how to rectify the situation.

Well, we were in an apartment with cupboards, and cupboards have contents, and so they were searched. Napisan, Fabuloso and Dash Active were all found and carefully considered.

Napisan was judged by The Keeper to be the most likely to be effective and he applied it not only to his water bottles but to mine for good measure.

For the next five days, our water had the underlying piquancy of nappies. We added fresh lemons to the mix and the water evolved into lemon-scented bathroom cleaner.

ENGLISH CHANNEL
HOME
Canterbury
Dover
Calais
Thèrouanne
Arras
Péronne
Laon
Reims
Châlons-en-Champagne
Brienne-le-Château
Bar-Sur-Aube
Langres
Champlitte
Besançon
Lausanne
Montreux
Col du Grand-Saint-Bernard
Aosta
Ivrea
Pavia
Piacenza
Fidenza
Fornovo di Taro
Berceto
Pontremoli
Lucca
San Gimignano
Siena
Bolsena
ROMA
BAY OF BISCAY
WE ARE HERE
ADRIATIC SEA
TYRRHENIAN SEA
N
S
W

DAY 54

Date: Saturday 25 August

Start: 07:30 at Piacenza

Finish: 17:20 at Fidenza

Distance: 39.3km (24.6miles)

Total: 1663km (1039 miles)

Daily average: 30.8km (19.2 miles)

A physical challenge often consists of 'type two' fun, when it is not great doing it but fun when you think back on it. Well, this day had a dollop of 'type three' fun thrown in. Not fun doing it and not fun thinking back on it. It was a head down, get the miles done day. And there were a lot of miles.

We realised that our hotel for tonight was not only 25 miles away but 25 miles in a straight line along a main road, the SS9. If we chose a safer route and meandered away from the main road, we would be adding more miles. For me, that was out of the question. If we were going to make up the time and keep to the schedule, we had no choice, we would have to walk the main road. So, we did.

We left Piacenza, walking through the out-of-town wastelands of carpet worlds and plumbers' depots, then continued, passing petrol stations, industrial sites, working farms, disused farms and more petrol stations.

We travelled over road junctions, under railways and alongside rivers.

It was a hard day: hard tarmac, hard traffic, hard walking. And then it rained – hard.

Our cherished belongings were instantly prioritised as we battened down our backpacks. Protecting the packs with high-vis orange rain covers, we were transformed into giant kumquats on legs.

In sheeting rain sent down from darkened skies, we got pummelled. And if the rain from the skies was not enough, from the roadside, the tyres of passing lorries slammed the fallen rain back at us with relentless accuracy.

On and on we pushed, getting more and more soaked, weighed down with water that wheedled its way inside every stitch of clothing. Eventually, reaching a bus stop with an awning and a seat, we took what shelter we could. Huddled together in a moment of respite we were somewhat taken by surprise when a bus arrived. Through my lank, wet hair, I looked at the driver sitting comfortably in a nice shiny bus. It nearly broke me. I so wanted to get on that bus, especially when I read it was going to Fidenza. I looked at The Keeper and he looked back at me, his eyebrows raised, not in admonishment but in question. Did I really want to get on the bus? I stood, tempted, so tempted, and then bravely, I waved the bus driver on. Wet through from my head to my knickers, unbelievably, what I really wanted was to walk from Home to Rome.

At that point, The Keeper did the best thing he could have done - he made me laugh. Taking his boots off, he tipped them up, expecting to release a dribble of water. To his surprise, a pint fell out, from each boot.

I was so surprised at his surprise (we were walking through a tempest, after all), that I giggled. And then, together, we realised the ridiculousness of it all. The only thing keeping us out that day was our stubbornness and our determination to walk from Home to Rome. Well, if that was our choice, then we needed to follow Nike's suggestion and 'just do it'. The Keeper retied his sodden shoelaces on his sodden boots, we picked up our kumquats, got back on the road and 'just did it'.

Eventually, the rain stopped, but we did not until we reached Fidenza and our hotel. I could do no more than collapse on the bed.

Noting my level of wear and tear and temporary paralysis, The Keeper went into action. I needed cleaning so he ran the shower and then gently stood me under the warm water. Patting me dry, he watched as I walked, monosyllabic, straight back to bed.

Turning his attention to the kit that needed washing, drying and sorting, he did both his and mine, hanging the clothes around the room to dry.

Knowing we both needed to eat but that it was unlikely I would make it to a restaurant, The Keeper went foraging at the local supermarket, returning to the room with his arms full of whatever nutrition (that was not in plastic) he could buy.

We sat in bed and ate supper, stylishly swigging Lambrusco from the bottle. Lambrusco had a certain nutrition, The Keeper reasoned. And anyway, it came in glass. We toasted to the fact that we had come this far and that was an accomplishment. Our adventure, after all, was just a journey of individual days, accumulated. We just had to get up and do it all over again tomorrow. *I can do that*, I thought, and, grateful to The Keeper and his Duracells, I fell asleep.

DAY 55

Date: Sunday 26 August

Start: 08:00 at Fidenza

Finish: 17:00 at Fornovo di Taro

Distance: 34.3km (21.4 miles)

Total: 1697km (1061 miles)

Daily average: 30.9km (19.3 miles)

Following that well-known recovery remedy of cheap wine and a solid night's sleep, we set off bright-eyed and bushy-tailed the next morning. What a difference a day makes. The tedium of yesterday's challenge was pushed to the back of the memory box and replaced by a beautiful day's hiking.

Fidenza is a small town and commune in the province of Parma. The heart of the town goes back to Roman times when it was an important staging point on the Via Emilia trade route. However, we walked out through its more contemporary suburbs. At some stage, these suburbs had benefited from considered town planning; it was appealingly laid out and a pleasure to walk through.

The pleasure continued as we left the plains and headed for the hills and the start of the Apennine Mountains. The Apennines stretch from Liguria to Umbria down the spine of Italy and are preserved in a series of national parks.

The lower slopes are mainly farmland, summer pastures and meadows of lush grass and native flowers. As the land climbs, the meadows give way to wonderful woodlands of beech, oak and pine. Scattered amongst the hills are ancient villages, with thousands of years of traditional life behind them. The villages are welcome islands of sanctuary to the hiker, especially if they have a restaurant or bar.

After a bit of a climb, our path took us near to the village of Costa Mezzana. Hot and thirsty, we decided to walk in and see what it had to offer.

It was Sunday and the melodic sound of a church service in full voice found its way to us. We paused to listen and admire both the singing and the church it came from. Then the need to quench our thirst with a cold drink pulled us to a bar nearby.

It was Oliver's Bar and Oliver greeted us warmly, bringing out his Via Francigena record book for us to sign and good-naturedly insisting on adding his own stamp to our Via Francigena passports. He congratulated us on our *camino* so far and asked with interest about our journey. As he placed our drinks on the table, he heartily slapped The Keeper on the back and wished us well.

It did not occur to us then, but we later learnt that his 'slap on the back' was a symbol of endorsement, a 'you are OK, go on your way' from a caring soul. From his stamp, we realised he was a traditional guardian of those who travelled the Via Francigena.

Our thirst sated, we left his bar to shouts of good luck and good travels from his less God-fearing, but not less hearty, congregation. These calls of encouragement, together with the melodic hymns from the church, followed us out of the village and back into the hills.

We finished our beautiful day's hike in Fornovo di Taro, where the only place open to eat was the local pizzeria. We arrived clean, full of enthusiasm and hunger, but that was not sufficient to get us into the dining room. Apparently, we should have reserved at birth judging by the look on the waiter's face.

We tried every charm offensive we had but to no avail, they had charm armour. Aloofly, they offered us a table outside.

"Will others also be eating outside?" I asked.

"No," came the reply.

We followed the waiter through the restaurant, passing table after table that was tantalisingly empty but presumably reserved by the more organised of Fornovo di Taro. Halfway across the restaurant we did a little shimmy and headed towards a tall stack of shelves. *Oh, good,* I thought, *the waiter has remembered a tiny table he can pop two unassuming hikers at.* Unfortunately not, he merely reached up and handed us down some blankets before opening the door.

We sat there in the dark and the cold waiting for our pizzas, The Keeper kindly wrapping more and more blankets around me as the minutes passed and the night grew even colder. Always approaching tasks with great energy, The Keeper applied so many blankets that I ended up looking like a larva, my head peeking out from a woollen cocoon.

I tried but failed to not look back through the window at the other guests in the warm restaurant that glowed with its own self-importance. Inside, the tables were beginning to fill, the chatter to rise. Friends and families were greeting each other, peeling off their coats and finding warm seats. Marooned and cocooned on our island terrace, two cold solitary souls on the wrong side of the window, I began to see the funny side.

"Do you feel a tad ostracised?" I asked The Keeper.

"I was just wondering where they would have put us if we hadn't showered," he replied.

DAY 56

Date: Monday 27 August

Start: 07:30 at Fornovo di Taro

Finish: 16:30 at Berceto

Distance: 33.5km (20.9 miles)

Total: 1731km (1082 miles)

Daily average: 30.9km (19.3 miles)

From Fornovo, we made our way uphill to the village of Sivizzano. It was a bit of a straggling village, the kind of place you are never sure where it begins or ends. Its claim to fame were the Angelus bells within its church, which apparently toll over forty times each morning at 06:00 and each evening at 20:00.

We were taking a two-minute break near the church when we were joined by a group of cyclists. We had met them the day before as they struggled to push their bikes up, and I was struggling to walk up a very steep and muddy track. They were a youth group plus two leaders riding the Via Francigena from Piacenza to Rome. They too had stayed the night at Fornovo but had sensibly eaten their own supplies for supper. Hellos were exchanged, and then, with a bit of a sheepish grin at the others, one asked what time we had started. We could see that he was, or rather they were, really asking, "How exactly did two old f***s get here before us?" We replied that we had left incredibly early, and they rode off content.

We were just leaving the village, climbing once more, when we came across an ancient wood oven on the side of the road. Typical to the area, this oven would have been used once a week to bake the bread for the family that owned it. Unused, it now sat as a reminder of the past lives and hard work of the people of the Apennines.

Our climb took us to the small and pretty village of Bardonne. Hot and thirsty, we headed straight to the village fountain and met up, once more, with the slightly surprised cyclists who had only just arrived themselves.

With all our water bottles refilled, the lads headed uphill, and we followed. The next village we reached was Terenzo. We were just coming into the village when, yep, we again encountered the cyclists. Well, half of them, as they had unfortunately mislaid a few of their team and together with one or two kind residents of Terenzo, were busy trying to find them.

We trundled off and hit an extremely steep gravel track. It was so steep that I got out the guide notes to check it was the right track. The notes said *from Sivizzano to Berceto is only 23km but it is probably one of the most strenuous and tiring stretches of the Via Francigena.*

If I had read this prior to doing it, I might have had a few misgivings, but ignorance can be bliss and now I had no choice. A few huffs and puffs got me ascending the track at a reasonable rate, or so I thought. But I could not keep up with The Keeper and his never ending Duracells.

"I'll see you at the top," I said and felt nothing but relief as I was left to climb in my own time. At the top, the track popped me out neatly at Casola where I found The Keeper seated at a bar which had fabulous views.

Sitting together outside the bar, enjoying a well-earned soda, our ears picked up the sound of multiple wheels on tarmac, accompanied by the puffs of their riders. Who should be coming along but the cyclists, all of them, thankfully. Their eyes popped out of their heads and the question 'what exactly did you have for breakfast?' rang out over the mountains.

Waving goodbyes, the lads headed off into the mountains once more. We stayed, finished our drinks and then also got back on the road. Our next target village was

OSTERIA BAR
al Birócc Artcafe

Cassio, where we aimed to stop for a quick bite. We were not the only ones. There on a patch of grass, tucking into huge sandwiches with enthusiasm, were the cyclists. The look of surprise and wonder at the two old codgers who had been shadowing them for the whole day was joined by a certain resigned acknowledgement.

After cheers and grins all round, we parted for the last time. Now that most of the climbing was done, the bikes were certainly going to be faster than feet. A huge relief to the group's confidence no doubt, which was, after all, what the leaders were trying to boost.

Having said goodbye to the group, we also said goodbye to the Alps. Whilst climbing the Apennines, our altitude had allowed us, on occasion, to savour epic views. We enjoyed huge panoramic vistas that lifted our spirits and laid the world at our feet. On one such occasion, 100 km to the north, we saw the Alps for the last time. We raised our hands in acknowledgement and bid them a fond farewell.

With the final climb done, it was downhill to Berceto, a charming town with fortifications, a cathedral and a multitude of potted climbing plants. The pots were everywhere, down every tiny street and at almost every doorway. Someone on the town council had green fingers or knew a good 'buy in bulk' deal when they saw it.

DAY 57

Date: Tuesday 28 August

Start: 07:30 at Berceto

Finish: 15:30 at Pontremoli

Distance: 32.2km (20.1 miles)

Total: 1763km (1102 miles)

Daily average: 30.9km (19.3 miles)

Leaving Berceto on a mix of wooded paths, tracks and a quiet road, we climbed steadily until we reached the pass over the Apennines of Passo della Cisa. Napoleon was responsible for building a road over this pass in 1808 as, prior to that, it had been a dangerous and lawless place. Pilgrims had been the common target of robbers but *not*, I thought, *today, unless any particularly suffered from anosmia*. It was hard and sweaty work climbing these mountains.

From the pass, we took a path adjacent to the road that wound its way down the other side of the mountain. In doing so, we passed a small, discreet cross identifying the place where two British soldiers had been shot by a firing squad in 1943. It was clean and tidy with a plastic flower at its base and even more poignantly, a picture of the two men. We stopped to pay our respects both to the soldiers and to the person who, commendably, still maintained the monument.

We were now in Tuscany, an achievement The Keeper and I celebrated with a quick sandwich. After a few more hours, we arrived at the edge of a hillside village called Molinella. As usual, we were hot and thirsty and, on this occasion, low on water. We needed a bar and, hey presto, there was one right in front of us. The door was open, its neon *aperto* sign illuminated and a drinks chiller in full view. All was looking good... apart from the person blocking the door.

Sitting in the doorway was an Italian mama. Her enjoyment of the culinary side of Italian life was evident as she struggled to contain her body within a barely visible white plastic chair.

We approached with smiles, but as we neared her chair, a torrent of Italian hit us full-on.

Getting a blank look from the two nitwits in front of her, the mama let rip again, this time accompanied by energetic gesticulations.

Wham went an arm out to the left; wham went the other out to the right. Two fingers were raised (*oh dear*, I thought), and a walking motion was made with them.

OK, got it, sling your hook, hikers. But we were thirsty, we needed water and that bar door was open. We retreated around the corner to discuss strategy. An offensive was clearly required.

Sent on reconnaissance a few minutes later, The Keeper discovered our obstacle to hydration had fallen asleep. Her head hanging forwards onto the natural pillows of her ample bosom.

We quietly took off our backpacks and, on booted tippy toes, crept past the Italian titan. We were just moving into position to help ourselves to drinks and leave the cash on the bar when a car came skidding to a halt outside. The mama awoke and we were caught, guilty, inside her bar.

Outraged, the mama continued where she had left off, accompanied by nods of her head and wobbles of her pillows. Thankfully, stuck fast in the chair, she was unable to physically reach us. But the younger man, the driver of the car, could, and he strode towards us.

"What do you want?" he asked in English. How had he known we were English?

He seemed surprised that, standing in his open bar, we should ask for drinks. However, he got them for us, but not glasses or ice, and we took the hint.

With drinks in hand, we gave the chair and its gesticulating owner a wide berth, picked up our backpacks and left, quickly. We were not sure what scenario we had either caused or observed. Whatever it was, we were not going to stay long enough to risk another *Mama Mia* moment.

Later that afternoon, we walked into Pontremoli, a small but ancient (when are they not in Italy) city dating from 1000 BC. It has long been an important pilgrim stopover, which is attested by the number of hospitals built locally. However, we gave these historical buildings a pass and stayed in a hotel with plumbing and a mini bar all to ourselves.

ENGLISH CHANNEL
HOME
Canterbury
Dover
Calais
Thérouanne
Arras
Péronne
Laon
Reims
Châlons-en-Champagne
Brienne-le-Château
Bar-Sur-Aube
Langres
Champlitte
Besançon
Lausanne
Montreux
Col du Grand-Saint-Bernard
Aosta
Ivrea
Pavia
Piacenza
Fidenza
Fornovo di Taro
Berceto
Pontremoli
Lucca
San Gimignano
Siena
Bolsena
ROMA
BAY OF BISCAY
WE ARE HERE
ADRIATIC SEA
TYRRHENIAN SEA
N
S
W
E

DAY 58

Date: Wednesday 29 August

Start: 07:50 at Pontremoli

Finish: 15:40 at Aulla

Distance: 31.9km (19.9 miles)

Total: 1795km (1122 miles)

Daily average: 30.9km (19.3 miles)

Today's route took us through numerous medieval villages, their names, such as Ponticello, Filattiera and Filetto, rolling off the tongue like varieties of pasta. Each of the villages were a wonder of aesthetics in their own way. Ponticello, for example, was a maze of stone vaults with buildings above. The vaults, differing in design between domed, barrelled and ribbed, were a testament to their long-gone craftsmen. They were also deliciously cool and quiet. The comings and goings of generations of villagers had worn a path in the flagstones beneath them and it was this that we followed from one end of the village to the other.

Between each of the villages, we had a series of minor diversions to amuse one or other of us. Along one country track, we came across my cousins (according to The Keeper): a herd of goats. They, and their two goatherds, were very amiable as they passed by, stopping for the odd scratch and nibble of my shorts. The goats, that is, not the herdsmen.

On another track, we had a singular encounter, that of a black snake as it slithered from one side of our path to the other. In surprise, I did my customary hip wiggle with an added foot jiggle, a move The Keeper found entertaining. Having encountered angry rattlers when we hiked the Arizona Trail, I knew this snake was a mere trifling. It still did not stop me, however, from keeping a good lookout for a few hours afterwards.

At one point, I had a chance for some retail therapy. An elderly white-haired gentleman, short in stature and wide at girth, was selling walnut shells over his garden fence. Not your average walnut shells but little gems that were hinged and opened to reveal intricate hand-carved nativity scenes.

Who could resist this North Pole renegade? I could not.

Through the chain link fence, the shopping began and I was shown a variety of shells from which to make my choice. Did I want one that included a hazelnut shell or not? The Keeper raised his eyes in disbelief. I made my choice. Mary, Joseph and baby Jesus inside a hazelnut shell, which was itself inside a walnut shell. My purchase was delicately wrapped up and presented to me.

I tucked it carefully into The Keeper's backpack, a memento of our time in the Apennines and a novelty from Santa's outlet store.

We spent the night in a hotel in Aulla and met up for a fun evening with Bob and Sandy, two friends who happen to have a home nearby.

DAY 59

Date: Thursday 30 August

Start: 07:30 at Aulla

Finish: 18.00 at Avenza

Distance: 35.3km (22.1 miles)

Total: 1830km (1144 miles)

Daily average: 31km (19.4 miles),

We shared our hotel breakfast and eagerness to be off with two coachloads of French tourists. They were keen to put their mass of numbers to an ordering advantage, but I was not in the mood. Taking up the challenge (and going directly to the kitchen), I managed to slip in our request of scrambled eggs before they had time to butter a croissant.

I sat in triumph as, first out of the kitchen, our eggs arrived at the table. The Keeper looked at me with *really?* written all over his face but then ate with the efficiency of someone who knew today's mileage.

An unusually gloomy day met us outside the hotel and things did not improve when, just out of the town, we had a steep climb up dirt and gravel paths.

By mid-morning, the gloom had turned to such hard rain that, seeing an old wooden farm building, we went in for shelter. A couple of the wall planks had fallen, and through the gaps, we had a beautifully framed view of a hilltop town in mist. Handily, we also had access to a large fig tree covered in perfectly ripe fruit. For every black cloud there is always a silver lining but sadly, in our case, not enough time to enjoy it fully. After a ten-minute break, during which we consumed more figs than is probably wise, we got back on the road and into the rain.

By lunchtime, the rain had stopped, and we had arrived at Sarzana in the province of La Spezia. The town's position on the boundary between Etruria and Liguria had given it military importance in the Middle Ages and had left it with both a citadel and a castle. The Keeper, however, did not give a scrumped fig for any ancient buildings that Sarzana might offer. Hungry, he was only concerned with what restaurants it had.

Lunch was eaten in a busy trattoria amongst the city's office crowd. We were surrounded by 'tucked ins'. Crisp white shirts were tucked into waist bands; laptops were tucked under chairs; feet were tucked under tables. We, on the other hand 'flapped'. Our sweaty shirts flapped outside our shorts; our stranded backpacks flapped on the floor; and our rain jackets flapped on the back of the chairs. I felt like a fish out of water and wondered how the 'tucked ins' felt about me. As the waiter stumbled over my backpack and mumbled disgruntledly under his breath, I came very close to realising the answer.

We did enjoy a delicious lunch though, and afterwards flapped happily on our way, ending up at the sea. Yes, the sea! The last time we had seen the sea, it had been the English Channel, and now we were at the Mediterranean. We had walked here! For one moment, neither of us spoke, we just stared at the water in triumph and wonder.

Recovering ourselves, we walked straight to the beach. To our surprise, we found a suburb on the sand. Mile after mile of beach had been subdivided into self-sufficient 'neighbourhoods'. Each area had its own identity, containing tastefully styled sunbeds, cabanas, bars and restaurants. Together they formed a chic but transient ribbon development of waterside luxury. We fitted in just fine - the open mouths of the vacationers illustrated that.

Having carefully picked our way through a multitude of Vilebrequin trunks and barely-there Missoni bikinis, we reluctantly left the sand suburb for a final slow drag to our B&B. We had started our day at 07:30 and eventually got in at 18:00. Over the last six days, we had walked 129 miles, but now the Apennines were truly behind us, and we were on our way to Rome.

DAY 60

Date: Friday 31 August

Start: 07:40 at Avenza

Finish: 15:00 at Pietrasanta

Distance: 26.8km (16.8 miles)

Total: 1857km (1160 miles)

Daily average: 30.9km (19.3 miles)

We returned to the sea and spent the morning walking along its edge, enjoying the scenery and salty air.

After a rather good seafood lunch, we packed up our theoretical buckets and spades, took one last look at the Med and headed inland towards Pietrasanta.

We were now in the province of Carrara, where local mountains are systematically sliced and sent to bathrooms and kitchens around the world. Surplus stock, it seemed, found its way to the local council; municipal art, water fountains, park benches and even curb sides were all made from beautiful Carrara marble.

From Pietrasanta onwards, friends were due to join us. The realisation was accompanied by a sudden desire for a new dress. That was going to put a spanner in the works.

“I need a new dress,” I shared with The Keeper. All went quiet; I could see he was struggling to understand this ‘need’. To him, the fact that I had worn my earth mother outfit for fifty-nine days straight could only mean one thing: by now, it was comfortable. Why would I want to change it? Shopping to The Keeper was as tedious as a trip to the dentist.

"Where are you going to buy one of those?" came the reply, whilst he indiscreetly looked at his watch. Had he forgotten my built-in boutique radar? Set it off and I can find a shop in a desert.

Within twenty minutes The Keeper was twiddling his thumbs outside a women's dress shop, and within forty minutes from announcement to attainment, the job was done. In appreciation and relief at the speed, the gallant Keeper offered to carry the extra weight in his own backpack.

Pietrasanta, which straddles the last foothills of the Apuan Alps, is a charming medieval town known as the 'Little Athens of Italy'. It has a long association with art and, of course, the working of marble. We arrived to find a selection of huge, contemporary busts installed as an exhibition in its main piazza. Luckily, the piazza was also full of bars, so we were able to appreciate the various big-heads from behind a beer and under an awning.

We were joined that evening by the super-fit Kenneth and Cathy. Freshly returned from Kenya and their latest ultramarathon (five marathons in five days sharing the wearing of a rhino suit!) they were looking forward to a bit of an Italian wander. We were looking forward to their company (if we could keep up with them).

DAY 61

Date: Saturday 1 September

Start: 07:30 at Pietrasanta

Finish: 16:00 at Lucca

Distance: 37.4km (23.4 miles)

Total: 1894km (1184 miles)

Daily average: 31.1km (19.4 miles)

Setting off the next day, The Keeper's unit was reformatted- it had a pacemaker, Kenneth.

The skies were rumbling with the threat of rain as we left Pietrasanta. A couple of miles later, they delivered on their threat and heavy rain fell. Wet through and with no obvious shelter, our only choice was to carry on.

At one point, our path took us up a steep track towards a village. The path began in a benign way but as we climbed, it narrowed and channelled the rain into a cascade of water tumbling down the hillside. We were puzzled, and understandably displeased, by the amount of water rushing past us; the torrent was now coming dangerously close to the top of our boots.

We were just below a road on the edge of the village when we came to the water's source. All the rain from the village's downpipes and its main road had been diverted to fall from one large pipe onto our path. Convenient if you were resident in the village or driving through it. If you were stupid enough to arrive on foot in a rainstorm, you obviously had to suffer the consequences. With no way around, our only choice was to go through, so we did.

Making it to the village bar, but not wanting to delaminate their seats, we all stood at the counter, water dripping from our clothes and puddling onto the stone floor. Getting soaked to the skin in Italy had not been on Kenneth and Cathy's summer agenda. However, as they stood in that bar, laughing at our enforced shower for four, they managed to top up our spirit of adventure, which had leaked a little. Rather like Cathy's shoes.

The skies cleared at 13:00 and mindful of his role, the Pacer pushed us on. We had 23 miles to do that day before we could reach Lucca, dinner and a bed.

Lucca was founded by the Etruscans and became a Roman colony in 180 BC. Its modern suburbia took a bit of getting through but, eventually, the medieval walls of the old town came into sight. These walls, once they lost their military importance, became a pedestrian promenade. You can walk around the entire perimeter of the city on them. Forget that, we were walked out and in need of a beer or two.

We entered Lucca through the San Donato gate and were met by a smiling 'Welcome to Lucca' guide. Even though she was missing the essential clipboard, she was still able to inform us of our hotel, bar and restaurant locations. Charlie, another hiking hero, was here!

Charlie led us along cobbled streets, past handsome piazzas and hundreds of tourists to San Martino Square. Here, in the shadow of the beautiful cathedral, we drank our much-deserved beer and poor Cathy attended to her much-in-need feet. They had not liked getting wet.

Dinner that night was at a fine trattoria, where we were also joined by the intrepid Nicola and Kevin. We had become a team of seven, and the team was heady with the excitement of the days ahead. As we shared the wine around the table, I realised we were also sharing something else: the adventure. And it made our own adventure all the more enjoyable for it.

DAY 62

Date: Sunday 2 September

Start: 07:00 at Lucca

Finish: 15:45 at Fucecchio

Distance: 33.5km (20.9 miles)

Total: 1928km (1205 miles)

Daily average: 31.1km (19.4 miles)

As planned, we met in Lucca under the Porta Elisa gate at 07:00. That is to say, six of us did, but one of us had accidentally slept through her alarm.

Fifteen minutes later, a ruffled Charlie arrived, admonishing herself profusely.

Charlie plays by the rules and eats all her greens; she works on the premise that if she is not ten minutes early, she is late.

Arriving fifteen minutes late was to her the ultimate sin and one for which she could not forgive herself. Erupting in self-reproach, she stamped her feet (I recognised that move) and said a few little F-words.

Stunned into silence at this outpouring, the group could do nothing but watch with sympathy (and relief that it was not them). The Keeper assured her it was 'absolutely fine' to be late for roll call, then demoted her from chief guide to mere foot soldier. I had a comrade.

Off we walked, heading towards Altopascio, thankfully mainly on tracks. This town was situated between what had been two marshlands and still had its Roman bell tower, used to summon travellers lost in the mist of the swamps.

Not lost ourselves, thanks to The Keeper's honed skills and the Pacer's interpretation of them, we left Altopascio and headed for Galleno.

As we arrived at Galleno, we met Marco and Frangipan (I'm sure that was not her name but as it sounded like that when she said it, it sort of settled on her). They were a young Italian couple who were on their way from Canterbury to Brindisi, a city in southern Italy. They hailed to us from across the road, immediately recognising kindred spirits and keen to share news from the road. After a quick natter, upwind of the couple, we parted company firm friends.

Walking on along the town's main road, we found a rustic-looking restaurant decorated in wood and red paint. As lunch was needed, we settled at a table. Despite yesterday's rain, Cathy mistakenly thought she was on holiday and asked for a beer. She revised her request as soon as she heard the gasp from others who knew the difference between a holiday and a Keeper's route march.

"Do you have low-alcohol beer?"

"*Si, si,* beer, little alcohol, I bring."

Three others of us also thought this was an excellent compromise and ordered low-alcohol beers. Out came the colas, iced teas, water and three of the tiniest bottles of beer: full alcohol strength, but little of it.

The owner, a bear of a man in local costume, joined us at our table. With gusto and great speed, he told us all about his restaurant and the many special dishes he could cook for us. We smiled and nodded our heads in politeness, but in fact, we were clueless.

Charlie, skilfully re-promoting herself to tour guide and translator, explained the rudiments to this slightly eccentric restaurant.

The owner, reappearing, treated us all to another soliloquy and stood, pen in hand expectantly. We ordered and the delicious food arrived. Any order that had met with his approval was correct. Any that had not, was not. Cathy and I, to achieve our five-a-day, had ordered plates of baked vegetables. What we received were two huge plates of meat and a smile.

Despite this, or perhaps because of it, the meal was delicious. As we left, the owner celebrated his skills as a chef and our enjoyment of those skills, by kissing all of us, several times.

The afternoon was spent in a happy haze of undulating off-road tracks, chatter and the occasional medic stop. Cathy's feet, showing their disapproval of yesterday's rain, had blistered today. Twice further, we bumped into Marco and Frangipan, and each time they were their smiley, if slightly off-scented, selves. It's hard to stay odour-free on the road.

Some hours later, Fucecchio and our hotel was a very welcome sight for all fourteen feet, but particularly Cathy's.

DAY 63

Date: Monday 3 September

Start: 07:30 at Fucecchio

Finish: 17:00 at Gambassi Terme

Distance: 38.7km (24.2 miles)

Total: 1966km (1229 miles)

Daily average: 31.2km (19.5 miles)

The Keeper's words 'it is always reassuring to have a boiled egg about your person', spoken halfway up a Swiss mountain, had morphed from a comment to a catchphrase. So, when boiled eggs were spotted hiding amongst today's breakfast buffet, a few of the cannier amongst us could not resist pocketing one.

Happy and full of breakfast, we left Fucecchio and ventured out into a countryside that felt like the Tuscany of holiday brochures. A lyrical landscape of rolling hills, idyllic hilltop villages and lines of Cypress trees.

After a couple of hours, just as we were beginning to feel the heat of the day on our backs, we came across a well-timed gift. A small stall had been set up for those walking the Via Francigena. Water, snacks, basic medicines and a freshly cut juicy melon were set out on a roadside picnic table: an anonymous kindness that we were all extremely grateful for.

As we enjoyed the melon moment, someone leant over an apartment balcony above us and wished us well. We, in return, asked for our thanks to be passed on to the Good Samaritan, not knowing if in fact we were talking to him.

We made our way to San Miniato Alto, which, as the name implies, needed a bit of a climb to get to. The town sits at the intersection of both the Florence-Pisa and Lucca-Siena roads. For centuries it has seen the flow of armies, traders and travellers. And today, it had us for a well-earned coffee. The brief coffee break over, we marched on, the Pacer out front, The Keeper working the maps, the troops trooping. Just after midday, we hit an eight-mile section of barrenness with no villages, therefore no cafes and no water. How seven adults could have arrived, surprised, at this point, beats me but there we were.

Lunch had to be scrounged from the hedgerows (mostly in the form of delicious fresh figs) and Cathy's backpack (a bag of peanuts was divided between us). And of course, for those of us who had snuck one, the boiled egg proved itself yet again. The catchphrase was turning into a mantra.

The drought ended at a bar in Borgoforte where we all nursed cold drinks, and a suffering Cathy nursed her feet, again. On the road once more, it was a hard-fought final climb up to Gambassi Terme. We each dug deep and did whatever we had to do to reach the town and our much longed-for showers.

Nicola put her head down and her mute button on and Kevin protectively stayed by her side. Putting my head down and disco on, I jiggled, wiggled and sang my way up. No one chose to stay by my side, and I cannot blame them.

With her feet in shreds from shoes that had done the dirty on her, the indefatigable Cathy did the only thing she could do. She threw those traitor trainers in the trash; in stockinged feet, she slowly and painfully limped in.

Showered and rested, we gathered as a group for dinner. This morning, The Keeper had dangled the day's mileage goal in front of us and, collectively, we had achieved it. We were united in quiet triumph. We sipped our aperitifs on the restaurant's terrace and watched the sun go down. With the cooling temperatures and the dwindling light, the land was mellowing and it was taking us with it. We chatted and laughed, relaxed with each other in a way that only a shared day of hard exercise makes possible.

DAY 64

Date: Tuesday 4 September

Start: 07:30 at Gambassi Terme

Finish: 15:15 at Colle di Val d'Elsa

Distance: 30.1km (18.8 miles)

Total: 1996km (1248 miles)

Daily average: 31.2km (19.5 miles)

With further Italian adventures beckoning them, which luckily involved more poolsides than hillsides, The Pacer and Cathy departed bright and early that morning. Lamenting our loss, the five of us set off for Colle di Val d'Elsa.

It was a beautiful, ethereal time to be venturing through Tuscany. The countryside was a palette of muted greys and an early morning gossamer mist hung low on the hills. The landscape, withdrawing from the silence of night, sat in a moment of quietness, waiting for the heat of the sun and the activity of day.

We stopped, compelled by the beauty, and gazed in admiration at the panorama before us. Then reluctantly, remembering we needed to walk through that landscape, we put our boots to the earth and moved on.

Amongst the hills, the outline of a walled city began to appear on the skyline. At first, it was a mere inconsequential dot, but eventually, the famous multiple towers of San Gimignano, a World Heritage Site, made themselves known to us.

The town is a medieval picture postcard and a honeypot for the eager tourist. For hours, it had just been the five of us trundling along the tranquil countryside and then, as we entered San Gimignano, it was not. We had to share our serene world with a great many

busy bee tourists, buzzing and bustling between monuments, shops and cafes. We were square pegs in round holes, sweaty, backpack-laden and not the least interested in olive oil or handbags.

We wound our way through San Gimignano's pretty streets and admired its ancient architecture. We left, however, content in the knowledge that, beyond its busy walls, there was a countryside at peace, and we were quite happy to be in it.

Choosing the all-important lunch spot democratically gets more difficult the more people there are. When it is just The Keeper and me, it works efficiently. I choose the spot and The Keeper agrees.

Kevin, seeking an alternative democratic method, diplomatically suggested we refer to the work of the American psychologist Abraham Maslow.

Maslow and his 'hierarchy of needs' were recruited to help us and eventually, decent shade, comfortable places to perch and a babbling brook were crudely achieved. Unfortunately, so were the unlisted insects and a great many of them.

We did not stay long, but it was just long enough for Nicola to consume not one but two large paninis. It would have been impolite for her supportive friends to comment on this growing appetite, so we merely rechristened her 'Two Panini'. After Two Panini discovered a unique way to soothe her foot ailments, and foolishly shared it with us, this name mutated into 'Two-Panini-Bidet'.

Although Colle di Val d'Elsa sits on the border with Chianti in the province of Siena, it is not known for its wine but for its crystal. A town in two parts, it is often overlooked by tourists as they pass through the more modern lower part. But on top of the hill are its antique origins and a rather quaint town.

As Charlie was staying in the lower part and we in the upper, we separated near her hotel with the understanding that she would join us for dinner. We then climbed, unexpectantly, for a further twenty minutes.

When we finally reached our hotel, somewhat tired, we decided that it was not a journey we could ask Charlie to do alone at night. As none of us fancied collecting her and doing it twice more, we asked the concierge whether we could arrange a taxi. "No, no taxis in this part of town," was the straight answer administered from a very straight face (that had a slightly turned-up nose).

Ignoring the nose, we explained our predicament to the straight face, but neither the answer nor the expression changed. Logic told me that this could not be the first time a taxi had been asked for at this hotel. Provision must have been made on some other occasion; it just needed teasing out, politely.

To commence the teasing, we started a sit-in. We took off our dirty backpacks and plonked them on the shiny marble floor. We took off our sweaty hats and placed them decoratively on the polished side tables and finally, we perched our grimy bottoms on the edges of their smartly covered chairs. That did it.

The straight face developed a discernible grimace, and the offer of the hotel car and driver was made more quickly than I expected. We must have been really grimy.

Having showered and changed, we asked to see the menu and to reserve the car for Charlie's homeward journey. "This is not possible," came the reply. "The driver will be finished for the night." Oh Lordy, our bargaining power for an alternative driver had gone down the drain with our dirt. We could not commence a sit-in, in clean clothes. What could we do?

A lovely young waiter stepped forward, "She can come home with me." What an offer! We agreed, in Charlie's absence, that she would be going home with the waiter. We also agreed to not mention the fact to her husband.

The waiter, it turned out, was a delightful and very respectful man from Honduras whose home happened to be near to where Charlie was staying. After sharing his life story during the walk down the hill, he left her, safely, at the door of her hotel.

DAY 65

Date: Wednesday 5 September

Start: 08:00 at Colle di Val d'Elsa

Finish: 17:15 at Siena

Distance: 34.8km (21.8 miles)

Total: 2031km (1270 miles)

Daily average: 31.2km (19.5 miles)

Today was the day we would walk into Siena, and we were all excited by the prospect. The four of us left our 'alta' hotel, rolled down the hill and picked up Charlie from her 'basse' hotel, before heading south and into the countryside.

The hillsides were embroidered with vineyards and olive groves, the occasional villa standing island-like amongst them. Walking mainly on small roads and tracks, we threaded our way through this landscape, going from village to village as we did so.

By mid-morning and with exceptional latte-timing, we arrived in the town of Monteriggioni. We headed straight for the piazza, a cafe and coffee.

This completely walled medieval town was built in the 13th century by the Sienese as a front line of defence in their wars against Florence. As a modestly sized version of San Gimignano, it is impressive but visited by fewer of the tourist bees. Over coffee and under the protection of awning,we were able to admire its historic buildings, including many of its impressive fourteen towers.

As we left the cafe, we each bought a panini for lunch and then turned a polite blind eye as Two-Panini-Bidet sneaked a second into her backpack.

Maslow was outdone when we came across a unique Via Francigena picnic spot. Someone had thoughtfully put together an outside lounge just for us hikers, complete with table, chairs, water and (oddly) a mirror. We were thrilled, even if none of us could face looking in the mirror.

Later that afternoon, The Keeper suggested a shortcut. I hesitated, having experienced these before. However, those goody two shoes, Two-Panini-Bidet and the Tour Guide, gullibly went for it. Ten minutes later, they were heard uttering the woeful line, "It will be better further on." Well, it was not. We all emerged scratched, grazed and a bit dazed, Two-Panini-Bidet (having originally supported The Keeper's suggestion) had learnt her lesson.

We arrived at the outskirts of Siena and had to negotiate our way into the centre alongside cars, vans, buses and bikes. The Keeper went up front to make 'eye contact' with the oncoming drivers, reasoning that if they acknowledged you, they were less likely to kill you. It must have worked as we all arrived safely in the old town.

Sometimes a place, rather than a person, can just grab you by your nether regions and make you gasp. Siena did just that to me. Declared by UNESCO as a World Heritage Site, it is a medieval masterpiece: a giant, vibrant, beautiful, open-air museum. Gelaterias, panetterias, boutiques and restaurants all bring it to life, jostling for attention within their medieval cityscape. We walked along its pedestrian-only streets, free from the worry of traffic, and fell under its spell.

We stopped at the famous town square, Piazza Del Campo, which was once the site of the old Roman forum. It is one of the most beautiful civic spaces I have ever been to.

The shape of the land moulds the square into a big concave shell. Thousands of red bricks, laid fishbone-style, cover the central ground and are further divided into a sunburst pattern by strips of travertine.

On one side the buildings are masterpieces of gothic civic architecture. Formed, like the paving, from the typical mellow red terracotta brick, they are occasionally sprinkled with embellishments of white travertine. At the lowest part is the town hall, Palazzo Comunale and beside it, standing out against the blue sky, the tall, slender tower of the Torre del Mangia.

A marble tabernacle, the Cappella di Piazza, built in thanks to plague survival, sits at the foot of the Torre del Mangia. Adding to the scenic drama, the splendid Gaia Fountain, formed from white marble, stands out against the paving.

On the other side of the square are the elegant palace facades built by the wealthiest families of Siena and, in front of them, the inviting terraces of cafes and restaurants for the modern tourist.

Once the setting for executions, bullfights and horse racing, the square has ceased the first two but still hosts the twice-yearly Palio horse race. Today, it also hosted a film crew.

Netflix was filming a car chase for a movie they were making. Over and over, again and again, they ran the same scooters, the same green car, the same black cars. I am sure the end cut would be no more than a few seconds long, but it was going to take hours to achieve it. After the first five minutes of screeching excitement, it all became a rather monotonous spectacle, a wearisome film set within one of the greatest settings in Europe.

Before The Keeper could get too distracted and start making 'eye contact' with the Netflix drivers, we moved on in search of our hotels. After walking through a maze of ancient side streets and alleyways, we eventually found ours, tucked away in an equally ancient building.

Dinner that night was in the heart of Siena, sitting on a fashioned terrace surrounded by the grand buildings of the city. We were celebratory for having reached Siena but sad with the realisation that, tomorrow, Charlie the Tour Guide would be going home.

DAY 66

Date: Thursday 6 September

Start: 07:15 at Siena

Finish: 15:30 at Ponte d'Arbia

Distance: 28.4km (17.8 miles)

Total: 2060km (1287 miles)

Daily average: 31.2km (19.5 miles)

Revisiting our tiptoeing routine, The Keeper and I made it out of the hotel for an early morning stroll. We could not resist another peak at the city before we had to haul on our backpacks and move on.

The quiet of the morning, before streets and buildings are cluttered and distracted by the comings and goings of humanity, is a great time to view any city. This morning Siena felt like it was ours alone.

We strolled up to the highest point in the city to see Siena Cathedral, reputedly one of the most important Romanesque-Gothic churches in Italy. We were not disappointed. Faced in a dichotomy of black and white marble, it is a magnificent building.

In the 14th century, there had been plans to increase the size of the Duomo and the new building work was started upon. Then, in 1347, the black death swept through the city, horrendously taking eighty per cent of its inhabitants with it. The building was never completed, and we could still see the half-finished walls of the Duomo Nuovo, left as a monument to not only Siena's ambition but also to its tragedy.

We were too early to go inside, but it was enough just to stand outside, to admire and reflect in the peace that comes with the early hours.

After collecting breakfast, Kevin and Two-Panini-Bidet, we walked out through the Porta Romana and regretfully left Siena. The countryside now had a more open feel, and we were often walking through arable land and alongside field hedges. The temperature was rising again and forcing us to take shade breaks whenever we could, wherever we could. For a minute or two of respite from the heat, we would stand side by side in the thin tracks of shadow cast by the field hedges.

I, by now, was used to these hedge moments, but it was not everyone's vision of a vacation staple. In those moments, I would look at our dear friends (hard-working doctors, who could have been sipping mojitos under parasols instead of warm water under hawthorn) and wonder how much longer they would remain our friends. But credit where credit is due, they kept smiling and kept going.

Lunch was taken in the second Via Francigena dining area we had come across. This time, it was just a fenced-off bit of grass beside the track, made by the kindness of someone towards passing pilgrims or hikers. We sat at a wooden table, on logs fashioned into chairs, with a myriad of chickens at our feet. Our sandwiches were valuable to us (especially to Two-Panini-Bidet), necessary calories to fuel us for the rest of the day. But it was hard to resist the clucking and general busyness of the appealing hens. Crumbs and crusts went their way, as they very well knew they would.

We were heading for Ponte d'Arbia and, worryingly, our second *agriturismo* hotel. The question of grimy sheets lingered in my mind (as I hoped their odour did not). Arriving in the town, we consulted the maps on our phones but could not find the road the hotel was on. Confused, we called our hosts and were told we needed to travel another mile or two outside of town. Another mile or two, in this heat, on foot? Oh dear, we had been here before.

I would like to say that 'we trotted off' to our hotel, but in reality, it was more 'we limped off', accompanied by a good dose of consternation. We walked alongside a railway line, down a farm track, over a bridge and eventually saw a hillock in front of us. We looked up and suddenly things were looking up. On the top was an appealing castle-like building, our *agriturismo* hotel.

On arrival, we discovered the hotel had a pool with parasols around it and a great view.

"This is more like it," beamed Kevin as they trundled off with their backpacks to find their room.

Within minutes, Kevin and Two-Panini-Bidet were living the dream, swimming in the pool and lounging under the parasols. For a few hours, at least, our friends had found their holiday paradise. I left them to it, walked across the lawn and went to sit in a summer house. Settling down in a cosy armchair, I looked back at the pool. Someone else, wearing nothing but a large smile and underpants, had joined them. Paradise lost.

DAY 67

Date: Friday 7 September

Start: 08:40 at Pont d'Arabia

Finish: 16:20 at San Quirico d'Orcia

Distance: 28.7km (17.9 miles)

Total: 2088km (1305 miles)

Daily average: 31.2km (19.5 miles)

Decadence was ours this morning. Breakfast was enjoyed at the heady hour of 08:00, and we then strolled, yes strolled, to the town of Buonconvento where, even though we had not gone far, we each indulged in a coffee.

Leaving Buonconvento in this relaxed state, we were lulled into a false sense of security and dropped our guard. When The Keeper chose to deviate from the route, I, like a simple-minded goat, just followed, and so did Kevin and Two-Panini-Bidet. We were 200m along the detour when someone called out to us that the Via Francigena was the other way. My goat ears pricked up, should we go back? The Keeper, however, replied to the local well-wisher that all was OK - he had a map. Having experienced these maps before, a few eyebrows were raised but not by The Keeper, and we pressed on. Right until we could not go any further.

With predictable inevitability, we were once again faced with the choice of retracing our steps or undertaking an uncomfortable assault course. In his defence, The Keeper tried to show us the map where, he assured us, there was a path marked. Someone (it might have been me) mentioned where that erroneous map could be rehoused.

Kevin and Two-Panini-Bidet accepted their fate and followed The Keeper into the undergrowth; the sucker that I am did too. It was not good, and plasters were needed when we eventually rejoined the Via Francigena.

Since leaving our home in the UK, we had passed many sites that tempted us to deviate from our path. The most consistently appealing of these were the vineyards. We had walked through the sunny slopes of grape-laden vines in England, France, Switzerland and now Italy. Apart from the cup of tea in the English vineyard, on every other occasion, we have kept our gaze firmly, if boringly, fixed on the path ahead.

But today when we passed by a Montalcino vineyard, and it was lunchtime, it felt different. The decadence we had started the morning with still lingered. And anyway, having noticed the 'wine and sandwich' offer, Two-Panini-Bidet was halfway down the drive, a woman on a mission.

We arrived at a smart, air conditioned tasting room, where another couple were already seated. Nodding politely, we headed to a table to sit down. What we had forgotten, in our haste to taste a Brunello, however, was us. The other couple were in possession of a Range Rover and an unassuming scent. We had neither of those admirable qualities and quite a few other, less admirable ones. We were quickly headed off at the pass by a member of staff. Standing in front of the table, she politely offered us the 'hikers' special', which also came with a table... outside.

Having been shown our place, we enjoyed some fine wine and sandwiches, whilst sitting under a lean-to overlooking the picturesque car park.

Whether it was the wine or the warmth, who knows, but the remaining section of the day's hike dragged on, our destination town seemingly remaining a mile or two away for most of the afternoon.

After a final long climb, we thankfully reached San Quirico d'Orcia. Like so many in Italy, it was another enchanting old town of narrow pedestrianised streets and colourful shop windows.

We found our hotel for the night and were met by the owner, Christina, who had a lot to tell us but only in Italian. As none of us spoke Italian, we tried French. With a shake of her head, we tried charades. We were just going through this painful process when an Italian guest arrived and offered to translate. Thankfully, the guest spoke English exceptionally well, with a perfect Brummie accent.

As Christina was not going to be there overnight or indeed in the morning, she wanted to tell us several things. As we were in Italy, she deemed the coffee machine to be the most important, so she started there. The Keeper was dispatched with the guest translator to stand in front of the sacred machine.

Christina: "*Questo è dove si mette l'acqua*," with the guest echoing, "Thees is where yow poot the water."

They both looked at The Keeper expectantly who, taking the hint, replied, "This is where I put the water."

"*Questo è dove si mette il caffè.*"

"Thees is where yow poot the coffee." Expectant eyes on The Keeper...

"This is where I put the coffee."

"*Questo è dove si mette la tazza*."

"Thees is where yow poot the coop." Expectant eyes again, followed by a "This is where I put the cup."

Kevin, Two-Panini-Bidet and I could only take it for so long. Barely able to make eye contact, we chuckled off to our rooms and left him to it. Twenty minutes later, having learnt the intricacies of the coffee machine, the breakfast buffet and the front door, The Keeper arrived at our room.

A 'thees is where you shouwer' from me was not met with a very polite reply from him.

ENGLISH CHANNEL

HOME

Canterbury

Dover

Calais

Thérouanne

Arras

Péronne

Laon

Reims

Châlons-en-Champagne

Brienne-le-Château

Bar-Sur-Aube

Langres

Champlitte

Besançon

Lausanne

Montreux

Col du Grand-Saint-Bernard

Aosta

Ivrea

Pavia

Piacenza

Fidenza

Fornovo di Taro

Berceto

Pontremoli

Lucca

San Gimignano

Siena

Bolsena

BAY OF BISCAY

WE ARE HERE

ADRIATIC SEA

ROMA

TYRRHENIAN SEA

N

S

E

W

DAY 68

Date: Saturday 8 September

Start: 06:30 at San Quirico d'Orcia

Finish: 15:15 at Radicofani

Distance: 30.1km (18.8 miles)

Total: 2118km (1324 miles)

Daily average: 31.2km (19.5 miles)

Whether we wanted one or not, we were each handed a coffee, made expertly by The Keeper, before helping ourselves to an early morning breakfast.

Since leaving Siena, we had been hiking through the Val d'Orcia, one of Tuscany's six World Heritage Sites, and today we would be going to Radicofani, which is at the most southern end of both the valley and the province of Siena.

Around San Quirico, the Val d'Orcia is an almost perfect Tuscan landscape. The quintessential aesthetic of rolling hills and ravines, oak forests, olive groves and vineyards.

It was another gorgeous misty morning and this perfect landscape looked freshly painted. It felt, delectably, as if we were standing in front of an expansive watercolour and were about to dip our boots into the colours of first light, into pools of grey and indigo paint.

We walked the 5km to the ancient village of Bagno Vignoni where thermal waters, having been found and bathed in by the Romans, have been in use (refreshed that is) ever since.

Where in most towns there is a main square, in Bagno Vignoni it is a giant, rectangular stone pool, from the bottom of which bubble up the warm waters. As it was still an hour or two before the average tourist greets his orange juice, we had the area all to ourselves. A quick dip in the warm water was very tempting. Would they really notice four frolicking hikers in the town pool? The Keeper thought not and went into action. He was just about to expose that night's laundry when I noticed a polite 'no bathing' sign. Should I say something? It was tempting not to; there was only the one sign. Then I noticed another, and it was in English. Damn. No frolicking for us after all. The Keeper reluctantly re-robed.

Thwarted from our thermal waters, we accosted a member of staff from the poolside hotel instead. The gentleman was laying out breakfast for his future guests, but we proposed that he make coffee for four disappointed hikers instead. He obliged and we commiserated our lack of thermal experience by watching the steam rise from both our coffee and the surface of the pool.

Reluctantly moving on, we spent the next few hours following tracks south, and as we did so the landscape became harsher and more barren. In the far distance of this tougher landscape, the distinct outline of a spectacular hill fortress sat on the skyline, its brooding watchtower black against the blue sky. Radicofani, our destination, had for centuries been one of the most important strongholds in Italy, protecting Tuscany from Latium.

Hunger eventually put us on the alert for a lunch spot. Our collective criteria were handsomely met when we reached some pools fed by the river Orcia. Hoorah, we could frolic after all. We sat on stepping-stones with our feet in the cool water and fed ourselves and the hundreds of little fish that gathered at our feet. All was calm when suddenly Kevin exclaimed, "Snake!"

Then, "No, hang on, eel!"

Sitting beside the water that flowed from the stream into the pool, Kevin had heard a large plop and then seen a rather disgruntled eel flop from one to the other. I pulled my feet out of that pool faster than chocolate is eaten at Weight Watchers. I did not mind the odd nibble at my toes from the darling little fish, but a disgruntled eel was another matter. Frolicking, for me, was off the agenda. The Keeper, with a bit more at stake than me, did not want to try his luck either.

As we drew nearer to Radicofani, we knew we were in for a climb and we were not disappointed, not in all the six miles of it. The four of us stayed together initially, but as we got more tired, our methods of coping differed. I wanted to crack on and get it behind me as fast as possible. Two-Panini-Bidet wanted to take it a little more slowly, to reserve her energy and her water for a steady climb. Recognising this, we parted at mile 3, each of the husbands deferring to the choice of their wives.

As The Keeper probably predicted, but knew better than to question, on went the disco. Singing and dancing my heart out to the amusement, and with the occasional accompaniment, of The Keeper, I boogied my way to the top.

Collapsing in the shade, I sat with The Keeper whilst we waited for our admirable friends to complete their ascent. Two-Panini-Bidet came into view, a picture of controlled effort, who, when she saw us, dropped all control and burst into tears. Our hearts went out to her, not sure whether she was crying from exhaustion or relief, or both. That climb was the finale to their Tuscan adventure and what a finale it was too. Through the tears, we noticed a smile: time to celebrate.

We walked into a town that was strung with flags and bunting and learnt that a procession was planned, the Palio del Bigonzo. The Palio is a two-day event which, as far as I could learn, involves young men racing around the town carrying *bigonzos*, containers used for holding eggs. Why they should do this was never clarified but then, why should they need a reason?

After the usual recovery routine in our hotels, we went into the town to investigate. We had arrived on the eve of the celebration, the night the members of the *Bigonzo* committee cook and the town eats, sitting together at communal trestle tables.

We were taken in hand and seated at a long table. A jug of red wine was plonked in front of us and then, as an afterthought, water arrived. Next came bowls of soup, then salad, then pasta, then meat, then dessert, then cheese. All were practically thrown at us with the enthusiasm of a committee who, having cooked the meal, was going to make certain it was consumed, if not savoured.

Halfway through the meal, a local lady, who had reached that age when wrinkle cream is more of a habit than a cure, took a shine to Kevin. Chatting at him with purpose and intent, she had Kevin backed up on his chair. Not understanding her words but understanding her meaning, Two-Panini-Bidet, The Keeper and I were looking on, amused at Kevin's predicament.

The locals, understanding everything, were in stitches. After a while and a little translation, Kevin, although flattered (and a little red in the cheeks), gently confirmed he was indeed a happily married man.

DAY 69

Date: Sunday 9 September

Start: 08:00 at Radicofani

Finish: 14:15 at Acquapendente

Distance: 26.5km (16.6 miles)

Total: 2145km (1341 miles)

Daily average: 31.1km (19.4 miles)

Kevin and Two-Panini-Bidet waved goodbye from their departing taxi with such vigour, I suspected the enthusiasm was not just for us. As well as their glorious feeling of fitness and achievement, I got an inkling that there was some relief in there too. The relief of the release, like the last day of school, or the end of the rectal examination. They did not have to get up today and do it all over again. Tonight, Two-Panini-Bidet would not need to soak her aching feet, hoorah! I think I would have clapped too.

As soon as the taxi left, The Keeper, as ever a results-driven man, threw me a bun and a smile and marched off. He had a schedule to keep. I stood for a while and watched as the last bit of the taxi went out of view, thinking of our friends and their return home. I missed home. And then I too got back on the road.

At the bottom of our descent from the village, where our path joined a dull main road, and my spirits might have dulled with it, we were met by two smiling and friendly faces. Much to our delight, friends Chris and Liz had decided to find us. Sneaking in a long weekend away from the children, Chris had realised they could modify their Tuscan break and walk with us for a while. I am sure that had thrilled Liz.

They had driven for an hour to meet us and then kept us fed and entertained for the two hours they were with us. They had then walked the two hours back to their car before driving the return journey to their hotel. What absolute stars. Especially as the terrain had not been interesting. I would have liked them to have experienced the painted Tuscan hillsides, far-reaching views and quaint villages. What they got was mostly dusty road-side tracks and the odd look from the odd sheep.

For the second time that day, we waved goodbye to friends, realising as we did so that the next time we would see a familiar face, we would be in Rome. We had left Tuscany and were now in Lazio (or Latium), Italy's geographical heart. Acquapendente was that night's destination and a bit of a climb away.

The name Acquapendente describes 'falling water' as there are several lakes and rivers local to it. However, that was for another day. Today we just needed to reach our hotel, which we did with some of the afternoon to spare. We made excellent use of our extra hours by doing nothing, thoroughly. I needed rest and sleep and even The Keeper, finally, succumbed to a nap and a recharge of his batteries.

DAY 70

Date: Monday 10 September

Start: 08:10 at Acquapendente

Finish: 13:15 at Bolsena

Distance: 21.9km (13.7 miles)

Total: 2167km (1354 miles)

Daily average: 31.0km (19.3 miles)

A comrade in arms to the 'apron' at Santhià was on duty at breakfast. Each crucial part of our meal was brought to the table singularly, as if the anticipation of its arrival were as important as the meal itself. It was not. I squirmed in my seat, patience at this point, I felt, being a virtue for only those who had a day's air conditioning to look forward to. I did not and I wanted to be on the road, making use of the cooler hours, not watching a solitary croissant crawl its way across the dining room.

The Keeper, knowing full well the extent of my patience with ineptitude, shot me a look. A look that, after decades of marriage, is as comprehensive as the spoken word. *Sit on your hands; go with the flow; and for goodness sake, Mountain Goat, don't let it get your goat*. I did as the look had suggested but not for as long as suggested. I could not hold out and went to pack my backpack, forsaking my croissant.

After the distraction of the slow tempo breakfast, it was a surprisingly relaxed and enjoyable day. The terrain was easy, mostly flat and green, with pockets of shade. We were in an agricultural area where the crops were potatoes, olives for oil, garlic, onion, cereals and grapes. The locals only had to throw in some tomatoes and lemons, and they had an exhaustive combination of menu options, right on their doorstep. Dessert, in the form of fresh juicy figs, was everywhere: on the roadside, field edges and garden hedges. Well-fed and regular (at least in September), not a bad combination for the locals.

We stopped for coffee in the town of San Lorenzo Nuovo, which is on the northern side of Lake Bolsena's crater rim. As we left the town square, we could just see a tantalising glimpse of cobalt blue water in the distance.

Lake Bolsena is in the province of Viterbo and, like many crater lakes, it is an oval shape. Although lesser known than some of its lake cousins (Lake Como, Garda or Maggiore, for example), Bolsena is the largest volcano lake in Europe. It has a circumference of 43km, and before the day was over, it felt like we had walked a good part of it.

As we descended from San Lorenzo Nuovo down to the lake, the landscape became less agricultural and more domestic. Holiday houses and communities dotted the lakeside and a main road circumnavigated it. We were trundling along this road, by now on the outskirts of the town Bolsena, when I finally had to admit that my beloved Decathlon boots, bought back in Reims, were wearing thin. I could feel the pavement through them. There was nothing for it but to swap them for my earth mother sandals, which, to reduce the risk of chafing, I wore stylishly over my socks.

Around the lake, outside of the medieval centre, Bolsena is a waterside Leamington Spa. Belle-époch houses abound, and patches of municipal land are enthusiastically planted. Arriving there in time for a late lunch, a gorgeous lakeside restaurant took our eye. We went in and asked for a table. The polite maître d' took our backpacks with care and, bless his cotton socks, he did not once look at my sandalled socks, which I hid under the tablecloth.

Learning from both the waiter and our phones that Bolsena was not the place to obtain new hiking boots, we headed to our hotel. Built in that difficult era of the late 20th century, when character was often forsaken for speed, our hotel lacked the charm of its older neighbours. This fact had not put the owners off, though, and with the apparent energy of weathermen in a tornado, they had added their own embellishments.

Urns, busts, statues, lions, pedestals and pillars were all over the place, and in exuberant excess, every window was hung with swags and tails. An eclectic mix of heady acquisition that was surprisingly successful at hiding the architecture. Turning right at Hermes and left at Apollo (or was it Aphrodite?), we found our room and realised the additions did not stop there. We would be sleeping with Venus de Milo looking on.

Hanging a towel over our new pal Venus, we walked back to the lake. It was early evening, and the sun was at its journey's end the far side of the water. We watched as the blazing orb, receding into the inky depths, sent a last ray of golden light across the water. It lit up all that was in its path: the water, the lake edge, the trees and buildings; even our own skin glowed. A departing life force that was reminding us, until its return, of its magnificence.

We felt at one with the world, our bodies strengthened from the exercise and our minds relaxed from the exertion. We found an outside bar and sat for an hour or two, our contentment not in need of conversation or activity to fuel it, just the lake, the fading light and a cocktail (or two).

DAY 71

Date: Tuesday 11 September

Start: 07:45 at Bolsena

Finish: 17:00 at Viterbo

Distance: 36.6km (22.9 miles)

Total: 2203km (1377 miles)

Daily average: 31.0km (19.4 miles)

Breakfast, in my book, is always important, but today it was especially so. As we had a particularly long hike ahead of us, representation from each of the food groups would be needed on our plates. With hope, we went in search of the hotel dining room.

After negotiating a myriad of multicoloured pillars and avoiding the fixed stares of the statues, we found the dining room and, to our delight, a fully laden buffet. Breakfast was expansive and, much to my relief, taken at our own efficient speed.

Nicely replete and nutritionally complete, we walked back into Bolsena from where we picked up the Via Francigena, skirted the lake for a bit and then turned inland proper. We were heading towards Montefiascone when we saw a road sign that made us smile, huge great ear-to-ear smiles that creased our faces and wrinkled our noses. 100km to Rome, only 100km to go. We looked at each other with the realisation that the end was within striking distance.

Montefiascone was, predictably, located on the highest hill of the local Volsini mountain range and as such, it was a bit of a climb up to it. Our path took us around the edge of the hill which, as we neared the town, followed the backs of tall, terraced houses and, at times, through their allotments. As well as a variety of herbs and vegetables, there were also numerous animal pens fashioned out of recesses in the mountain or made from piled local stones. We clucked at hens, oinked at pigs and bleated at my goaty relations as we passed by.

Having established that hiking boots were not sold in Montefiascone and ankle socks with sandals were the fashion for today, we set off for Viterbo. Our route took us across the countryside and down dusty country lanes. It was hot; we were thirsty; and I was beginning to fantasise about ice-cold drinks when up ahead I saw a mirage. In the middle of some fields were a group of scantily clad individuals having fun. Some were on loungers, some splashing about in water and some, more importantly, eating ice creams! "Are they for real?" I asked The Keeper. But why here, down a dusty track in the middle of a field?

Nearing, we realised that the sparsely clad splashers were enjoying natural thermal pools. Well, they were welcome to the water, but I very much liked the look of their kiosk. Minutes later we sat rapturously happy, slurping cold drinks and licking ice creams. Both parties, splashers and hikers alike, amused and intrigued by the improbability of the other.

Since its heyday in the Middle Ages, Viterbo has not seen much development and is off the usual tourist route. Consequently, it has one of the best-preserved medieval centres in Italy. Trying to find our B&B was a delight. We walked down tiny lanes, across ancient squares and in front of original stone houses.

In one such square, Piazza del Gesũ, and at one such stone house, we found our B&B. Sympathetically refurbished in a contemporary style, the building was owned and run by an architect with an intriguing story. Each year, the town of Viterbo undertakes the Macchina di Santa Rosa. a hundred men carry a 30m high, 5 ton tower, for 1km through the town. The procession attracts thousands of visitors and is on the UNESCO list of intangible cultural heritage. Our host had designed the current tower and this year's procession had been just eight days earlier. It must have been an amazing sight.

We went out to dinner in the square and sat under the strung lights of the local restaurant. The night was warm, the wine palatable and delicious aromas were making their way to us from the kitchen. I was just deciding whether to order the fish or the chicken when, *crack*, the chair leg snapped, and I was suddenly served onto the floor. From beside the table to under the table in less than a nanosecond, I was a stricken heap of goat.

The waitress came running over; I could see her shoes approaching on the flagstones. *Oh good*, I thought, *help on the way*. She bent down and rescued... the chair. Leaving me under the table, she held the chair aloft, as if to say to her other customers, *it is OK, she is not drunk, she's just too heavy for the chair*! I was not sure which of those I preferred.

The Keeper came around the table and lifted me up; another chair was found; and I was hastily re-seated. Dinner was quieter than expected and overnight, I grew an impressively large bruise on my behind.

NON METVENS

DAY 72

Date: Wednesday 12 September

Start: 07:40 at Viterbo

Finish: 16:00 at Capranica

Distance: 35.3km (22.1 miles)

Total: 2239km (1399 miles)

Daily average: 31.1km (19.4 miles)

As I dressed this morning, I realised I had a choice in the footwear department: boots that gave me the persona of a hiker but less protection than a bowl of blancmange or sandals and socks and the persona of a librarian on holiday. I plumped for the bibliophile fashionista and, putting on my sandals, I added a wish that my footwear would last long enough to get me to Rome.

After negotiating another myriad of ancient and delightful buildings, we eventually left Viterbo on a surprising road. It was a single lane with barely any space either side and banked by high walls of cut earth. These walls, at three times our own height, created an eerie, tunnelled experience, within which we could just see a sliver of sky above us. We walked along, hoping not to meet a car, or if we did, that there would be enough space for it and us.

With the cutting finally over and the world open to us once more, we spent a good part of the day bobbling along towards Capranica. As we neared our destination the farming changed from general arable to one specific crop: hazelnuts. About thirty per cent of Italy's hazelnuts come from this area, and we walked through huge plantations of them. Acre after acre of neat lines of hazelnut trees with carpets of shed nuts on the earth beneath.

It was harvesting time, and the nuts were being collected off the ground by giant ride-on vacuum cleaners driven by masked men. The men were friendly enough, nodding or waving as they passed by, giant dust clouds chasing behind them.

The front part of the hazelnut harvesters had multiple sweepers that channelled the nuts beneath the machines. Then, through large, tentacle-like hoses, the nuts were sucked up and deposited into trailers. Trailer after trailer were then driven off to some distant point for processing. The nut groves continued right to the very edge of Capranica, every bit of land planted to feed the world's Nutella habit. We moved from beside nut trees to beside tarmac in a matter of metres.

Capranica is on a hill that overlooks the Sutri valley and is on the Via Cassia. Since Siena, we had been keeping company with the Via Cassia, a historic and once-important road that led from Rome to Etruria. Built by Cassius Longinus in 107 BC, it follows the hills and visits such towns as Viterbo, Bolsena and Lucca. Today, it ran alongside the town walls on an escarpment and brought us right into the old part of town.

As was usual after a 20-mile day, we were hot and weary and hoping to find our accommodation easily. We found the right address; a narrow street with large, ancient buildings facing each other. There was a local hospital (with a few inmates sitting on benches outside), a hotel and a bar but not the slightest whiff of our place, Apartment 17.

With the inmates watching, their heads following in unison, we walked up the street. Still no sign of Apartment 17. We turned and walked back down the street, all the heads following. Again, still no sign of our building. With all the heads fixed on us, we walked back up to the bar. This was turning into Wimbledon, and we were the ones on centre court. We asked the waitress in the bar if she knew where Apartment 17 was but received a blank stare before she added the afterthought of, "Try the hotel."

We walked back, past the spectators, to the hotel. No, they did not know where, on this single street, we were due to be staying. We called the contact phone number, which rang, but no one answered. We walked back to the bar, past the turning tennis heads and regrouped over iced tea. Paying the bar bill, I tried a different approach with the waitress we had quizzed earlier. "Do you have the keys to an apartment near here?"

"The apartment opposite? The one with the white door and no number? Yes, here they are."

Hallelujah, we were in. We walked across to the apartment and, turning, I gave a thumbs up, as if I had just hit a winning backhand slice across court. The tennis heads gave a celebratory cheer.

Supper that evening was in an ancient building off an equally ancient street, which was accessed through an ancient arch. Luckily, the food was not ancient at all but fresh and tasty. It was cooked by the third generation, and served by the fourth generation, of the original owners of the trattoria. Priceless.

DAY 73

Date: Thursday 13 September

Start: 06:40 at Capranica

Finish: 14:20 at Campagnano di Roma

Distance: 32.2km (20.1 miles)

Total: 2271km (1419 miles)

Daily average: 31.1km (19.4 miles)

Over the course of our adventure so far, we had learnt to temper our expectations ahead of each night's accommodation. We did find however, that a few basic things, such as a showerhead, a fixed toilet seat, a kettle or coffee machine and cups always came in useful. As Apartment 17 not only lacked its door number but also these finer details, we had experienced a rudimentary night and opted for an early start.

And how fortunate that we did (there is always that silver lining). As we stepped out of the apartment, we realised that a monumental spectacle was occurring silently above us. We could only stand and look up, arrested by a sky that engulfed us in colour and wonder. All around us, the buildings were a brooding unlit black but from behind them, to the east, the sky was on fire. From its golden heart, reds and oranges swept out in intense flames of pigmentation. Emerging from this intensity, wings of crimson flew across the sky, eventually cooling to pinks and blushes of salmon, until finally, in the distance, a soft lilac lapped at the edges. It was mesmerising and made more poignant by its ephemerality.

Energised, we headed off for breakfast three miles down the road in Sutri. Picturesquely sitting on a narrow hill surrounded by ravines, Sutri is a fortified town of Etruscan origins. Its old town of medieval buildings dominates the skyline, but it was the more ancient ruins to the south that really interested us.

An amphitheatre, a necropolis and Etruscan cave tombs were all discovered before breakfast. We stopped to take a closer look at the enormous and well-preserved elliptical stadium built by Emperor Augustus. So much of the original building still stood that we could almost hear the Romans cheering from their tiered viewing points.

Leaving Sutri, we put another solid 10km of small roads and tracks behind us. The local fields were still dominated by hazel groves, and I was beginning to develop an uncommon desire for a Nutella sandwich.

Reaching the next town of Monterosi, whilst the Keeper took a call, I went off in search of a bar, coffee and if I was lucky, my sandwich.

Seeing a bar, I also noticed an unmistakable group of pilgrims clustered around one of its tables. Backpacks were on the floor, maps on the table and bodies, sun hats and scarves draped over chairs. Instant recognition amongst the species meant conversation was immediate and the invitation to join them almost as soon. I sat down to chat.

They were the United Nations of pilgrims, a group of five from five different European countries. Whilst they had all started singularly, they were now either walking together or bumping into each other along the way. Unlike The Keeper and me, none were walking the whole Via Francigena in one go.

Hans, from the Netherlands, was walking the entire route but in stages over several years. He was a tall, slim gentleman with an inquisitive mind and a need to be correct.

The usual questions opened the conversation: where did we start? When did we start? How heavy were our packs? Hans, incredibly polite, started to look a little sceptical at my replies. He quietly brought out a little blue book and began to scrutinise me.

"Did you walk from Piacenza to Fidenza in one day?"

"Yes," I replied.

He discreetly looked in his book, raised his eyebrows and said, "But that is over 40km!" His little blue book, I realised, meticulously recorded the mileage and elevations of each of the stages.

He consulted his book again. I felt like I was under interrogation; if I gave the wrong answer, would I be taken out the back and shot?

"Did you walk from Bolsena to Viterbo in one day?"

"Yes," I answered.

Up went the eyebrows again. "But that is 36km," he commented.

"I know," I could not resist answering. "I walked it."

Hans was obviously having a hard time coming to terms with my answers, and I was beginning to worry about the firing squad. So, when having finished his call The Keeper joined us, I swiftly introduced him to my new friend. Hans moved his interrogation from me to him and with relief, I tucked into a croissant (with Nutella on the side).

By the end of the coffee, Hans had one final question. "How many rest days?" he asked.

When we replied 'none' he put down his notebook, and with a slight nod of the head and a big smile, he said, "OK, so now I know that you are nutters." *An appropriate choice of words for this part of the world*, I thought.

After saying farewell, we headed off again, walking on mainly dirt and gravel tracks. It was undulating countryside, and the further we ventured, the more conventional the farming became until, by lunchtime, there was not a hazelnut tree in sight.

Lunch was eaten by a waterfall, in the cool of some riverside trees. Just as we were leaving, someone further along the river began playing a clarinet, a melodic, wistful piece that drifted downstream to us.

We walked up the river, listening to the haunting music, getting nearer to its source with each step. Eventually, we saw a simple wooden hut, set back from our path. The hut did not have windows, but its door was wide open, and it was from here that the music emanated. Why someone was playing, or for whom, we will never know, but for us, it was a memorable gift.

At the end of our day, we had a steep climb up into Campagnano di Roma, a municipality in the Metropolitan City of Rome. We were now actually within the wider city of Rome. It was a very pretty town, medieval and full of sinewy streets to navigate. Compared to the day before, finding our apartment was delightfully easy and, as it had a keypad (and we had the code), delightfully easy to enter.

DAY 74

Date: Friday 14 September

Start: 07:00 at Campagnano di Roma

Finish: 13:00 at La Storta

Distance: 24.2km (15.1miles)

Total: 2295km (1434 miles)

Daily average: 31.0km (19.4 miles)

Within a day of lasts, Campagnano would be the last town we would wake up to outside of Rome. We would venture along our last 'Keeper's alternative route', and it would be the last time I would play swapsies between my boots and sandals. Later, we would do the last kit wash.

We left our apartment and Campagnano and were surprised that there was still plenty of countryside, despite being so close to Rome. The countryside eventually became a protected area, the Veio Park, a huge 15,000-hectare green lung for the citizens of the capital.

Our first stop was the town of Formello where, over cold sodas, The Keeper put forward an alternative route he had seen on the map. The route was only a couple of kilometres long but would save half an hour. Should we do it?

The Keeper is a glass-half-full man with a long memory for success and a short one for failure. In fact, he does not have failures, only problems that in one way or another get resolved. Add that to my general level of weariness and the temptation was too great We jointly agreed to take the alternative route.

Off we trotted, our chosen route taking us away from green land and along suburban roads, which is not ideal but judged acceptable if it meant making up a few klicks. We were doing rather well when, rudely and without notice, our road came to an unscheduled, unmapped dead end. Predictable, I suppose. Being rather familiar with the concept of 'dead' after seventy-four days on the road - dead tired, dead on our feet, dead meat to mozzies - we decided that to turn around would just be dead wrong. We needed to keep going, dead ahead. But how? This was not a failure, just another problem that needed resolving.

The Keeper pointed out that the road we needed to be on was, tantalisingly, just the other side of a large patch of scrap land. Scrap land that was undoubtedly a prized building plot for someone and as such had a surprisingly sturdy fence protecting it. We were just contemplating what to do when a handy hole in the fence caught my eye.

Discreetly, I nodded my head towards the hole and raised my eyebrows of communication towards The Keeper. In return, he nodded his agreement, looked furtively around for any observers, then handed me his backpack. Practising some impressive yoga moves that I had never seen (or heard of) before, The Keeper managed to squeeze through. Pushing both our backpacks after him, I followed, commando-style, on my elbows and knees. I have never been good at yoga.

We had done it now. We were on the wrong side of the fence, and probably the law, but our objective was within striking distance. We started to make our way across the rubbly, thistly ground as fast as we, and two backpacks, were able. I was at this point thankful that my feet were sporting my boots, giving me marginally more protection than my sock and sandal ensemble.

Keeping close to the boundary fence, we were one-third of the way across when we passed a sign that did not need translating. It was a picture of a dog which, from his open mouth and bared teeth, was more Brutus than Fluffykins. Interesting.

We were halfway across when we heard snarly barking coming from somewhere behind us. Interesting had been elevated to worrying.

We were two-thirds of the way across when we heard men talking and more snarly barking. A few little F words slipped from our lips.

Our boots found wings, and we sprinted to the other side, hitting the fence between us and our road. Our eyes searched for an escape hole, any hole, but we could not see one. Damn, damn and triple damn.

We ran along the fence, checking and double-checking, but there was nothing to climb through or over. We had come this far, was it all really going to end in some rubbly field, torn from our task by the teeth of a Brutus or two?

And then I saw two posts standing side by side. If I pulled at one of them hard enough, I might just be able to create enough space for us to pass through. I pulled and pulled but, nothing happened.

I heard the men and the snarly barking and pulled again. This time, with the strength of someone whose bottom was right on target for a full set of canine gnashers, a small gap appeared. The Keeper ran to me, we took off our packs as fast as our fumbling fingers could manage and threw them over the fence. The Keeper pulled the post, and I squeezed through a gap no wider than a Chinese noodle on a diet. The Keeper pushed an arm through, then a leg, then, with a pop, his body was roadside. Never so pleased to see a road and traffic, we pushed back the post and made a sharp getaway.

Eventually stopping to catch our breath, we shared a look of amused recognition. We were silly old duffers with less sense than a submarine with screen doors.

But I also caught something else in The Keeper's eyes; an extra glint of mirth. Oh no. I was willing to share his obvious enjoyment of the canine caper, but I was not going to encourage more of them. My heart could not take it and, anyway, I needed to secure the future safety of my bottom. Rather primly, I heard myself saying, "That's the last time we are taking any more of your shortcuts." When that did not provoke the response I had hoped for, just another chuckle, I added "Ever," which made me sound like a five-year-old. In frustration, I walked on, with The Keeper suppressing his amusement behind me.

With no further incidents (or shortcuts), we arrived in the vicinity of our hotel in La Storta. We had been walking along a busy road and needed to take a side road to reach the hotel. At the turning was a bus stop, and I glanced at the timetable. Buses went from there straight into the centre of Rome. Oh, how tempting, it was lunchtime and only 20km into Rome. We could just nip in. The Keeper looked at me. He knew full well what I was thinking and why. Our family was assembling in Rome that afternoon, and I missed them all. We both missed them.

I realised we were having another defining bus stop moment, but thankfully not in the pouring rain this time. The Keeper asked if I wanted to get the bus into Rome. I thought about it. The longing to see the kids was real. But did I want to spoil our last day by doing it hurriedly tonight? No, we had agreed to meet them outside the Vatican at noon on 15th September 2018, and that is what we were going to do. I shook my head. "Let's find the hotel."

It was not the most inspired accommodation for our last night, hovering in that no man's land between form and function. The potted palms, suffering an identity crisis in the corner of the foyer, were not sure if they were enhancing the decor or serving as ashtrays. Judging by the debris in their pots, I think the guests had decided for them.

Having negotiated the stairs and the wrong set of room keys, twice, we achieved our sanctuary for the afternoon and night. With enthusiasm, we set about our final preparations. We washed our kit thoroughly and cleaned our boots too. Nothing was greatly improved by the attention, but at least it was clean.

We emptied everything out from our backpacks and cleared the detritus from a life on the road. There was a hotel shampoo sachet (half full), a disgusting oily insect repellent and a split tube of antihistamine. Old bits of map, a couple of information leaflets on national monuments and squashed after-dinner chocolates given out with restaurant bills and kept for energy emergencies. Lurking at the very bottom, there was the odd peanut (fluffy from the fibres of the odd tissue) and the odd tissue. In every seam edge, burrowed as if seeking refuge, were the breadcrumbs from untold sandwiches.

Having thrown the detritus, I looked at our remaining assembled items. There were not many of them, and yet they had been all we had needed for the last seventy-four days; each one had a purpose and was valued for it. We had successfully reduced our worldly goods to how little we could get away with, the antithesis of consumerism. It had not affected our happiness. In fact, it had enhanced it and freed us to do what we love. As I repacked my backpack, I was grateful to every piece I handled, even the earth mother outfit.

With our jobs done and naps taken, we still had a bit of time in hand. My body by now had an ingrained fatigue, so I was quite happy to gently while away the late afternoon reading the news and writing my blog. The Keeper, however, as we all know by now, is not a sitter. The need to always be active is often exhausting, not for him, of course, but for those around him, which at that precise moment was me. I suggested he went in search of nutrition. Finding a local supermarket, The Keeper returned with fruit, salad and more fruit, in particular grapes, helpfully pre-pressed into a Prosecco bottle.

With some bubbles inside us and The Keeper finally parked, our emotions rose to the surface. Tonight would be our last night on the road. Our last experience of simple living, when our daily concerns stretched no further than what we would eat and how we would stay cool or warm or dry. This was our last night avoiding the hectic tempo of normal life, the clocks, the schedules and the agendas that had all been put aside in favour of the pleasure of the present. We had reduced the pace of our lives and in return, we had gained a sense of contentment both in our minds and our bodies.

When Hippocrates had said 'walking was man's best medicine' he had hit the nail on the hiker's head. That evening, as we sat in our hotel room, we realised another last: tomorrow we would take, for a while anyway, our last dose of daily medicine.

We finished our Prosecco and went to bed. Enough philosophy for the night, Rome and family were calling.

ENGLISH
CHANNEL
HOME
Canterbury
Dover
Calais
Thérouanne
Arras
Péronne
Laon
Reims
Châlons-en-Champagne
Brienne-le-Château
Bar-Sur-Aube
Langres
Champlitte
Besançon
Lausanne
Montreux
Col du Grand-Saint-Bernard
Aosta
Ivrea
Pavia
Piacenza
Fidenza
Fornovo di Taro
Berceto
Pontremoli
Lucca
San Gimignano
Siena
Bolsena
BAY OF
BISCAY
ADRIATIC SEA
WE ARE HERE
ROMA
TYRRHENIAN SEA
N
E
S
W

DAY 75

Date: Saturday 15 September

Start: 07:30 at La Storta

Finish: 12:06 at Rome

Distance: 25.4km (15.9 miles)

Total: 2321km (1450 miles)

Daily average: 30.9km (19.3 miles)

I awoke to the realisation that today, The Keeper and I would walk into Rome. Excitement coursed through my body (which is not good at my age) and sent me running to the bathroom, which woke The Keeper, which meant we were up for the day. And it was early.

Convincing the hotel staff to serve us breakfast at 06:15 had been a challenge that we overcame with polite determination and a dollop of the bravado we picked up somewhere in northern Italy.

Backpacks on and ready to go, we strode out onto the Via Cassia. Having played footsie with this road since Siena, we had seen it in all its guises. Today, it was a busy suburban road, lined with pizza, kebab and tyre shops. A far cry from the romance of the Tuscan hillside, where it winds its way through olive groves, but strangely familiar never the less. We stayed on the Via Cassia until we reached the junction with the Grande Raccordo Anulare, Rome's version of the M25. The journey so far had been longer than advertised in the guidebook and we began to suspect that the suggested 9 miles on foot was going to be stretched out. Thank goodness we had started early.

As soon as we were over the motorway, we turned down a lane that looked like a private drive. We paused, concerned, but reassured by a Via Francigena sign and our guidebook, we continued. A few minutes later, a white soft-top Mercedes stopped beside us. "Are you lost? Where are you going?" asked the woman driver in a tone that really implied, *should you be here?*

Our reply of 'no, we don't think so, and we are going to the Vatican', created a lurch of the car. That stumped her. Realisation dawning, she asked, "Are you *pellegrinos*? Where did you start?"

"Yes. England," I replied, wondering if this woman ever asked a question singularly.

"Congratulations and well done," she replied, continuing to speak in double tongue.

Unable to resist, I added the reply, "Thank you, and thank you."

The lane took us to Insugherata Park, an important naturalistic corridor that connects the built-up edge of town with the Veio Park. It was fascinating to walk through such an unmanicured conservation area so close to a major city. For part of the way, we crossed grassland, then we followed the Acqua Traversa alongside the willows and poplars that grew on its banks. Eventually, we turned uphill away from the river and walked through a woodland of oaks and chestnuts, before leaving the park for the Via Trionfale.

The pizza, kebab and tyre shops on the Via Cassia were replaced by a multitude of low-rise apartment blocks on the Via Trionfale. The commodities of family life and city living (washing, bikes and tomato plants) all jostled for space on the numerous balconies.

Still following the guidebook, we eventually turned off the Via Trionfale and took a couple of left and right turns. The area, increasing in wealth, had now exchanged apartment blocks for single dwellings. We then went up the Via Lego and along the Via della Camilluccia, before finally taking a left down Via Edmondo De Amicis. Now we knew for certain that it was to be a longer day than advertised. By our reckoning, the 9 miles would be nearer to 15. Our family was gathering to greet us at noon,The Keeper, hating to be late even after seventy-five days, kept a close eye on his watch.

Some tall, ordinary looking metal gates announced the entrance to the Monte Mario Park. Monte Mario is the highest hill in Rome, although, as it is just outside the city boundaries, it is not one of the proverbial Seven Hills of Rome. Part of it is residential and part of it conserved as a nature reserve.

As we walked up the hill, we saw a fellow pilgrim ahead, a pleasant young Frenchman whom we had met ten days ago. He was walking from Paris to Rome and as he carried a tall stick, we had referred to him, with untold imagination, as 'Stick Man'.

"Hi there," we called out.

As he turned, his mouth fell open and out fell, "What are you doing here?"

Odd, I thought, *I should think he knows exactly what we are doing here. We walked, just like he did.*

Recovering, he gave us a great big grin and his eyes twinkled with amusement. "Do you know, I have been walking really, really hard for the last week. I thought you two would be way behind me, and then here you are. It is a surprise."

Then, together, we turned to a lookout point and all three of us were suddenly muted.

There before us, laid out in all its magnificent glory, was Rome. From our viewing point, we had a perfect south view that spanned across from the Tiber river to the Vatican palaces. In one panorama, we could see most of the ancient monuments of the city which, of course, having ascendency over them all, included the great St Peter's Basilica.

It took our breath away. We grinned at each other. Out came the phones and pictures were taken of each other, with each other, of the view, of Rome.

Wishing us *bon courage* for the final leg, and as if proving a point, Stick Man then sped off. We looked at our watches and decided that if we too got a wiggle on, we could just make it to the Basilica for noon.

Seventeen switchbacks took us dizzily off Monte Mario and after a couple of side roads, we were on the Viale Angelico. We were now about 2km from the Vatican. We would make it; after seventy-five days, we would be bang on time to meet the family. The Keeper was quietly triumphant.

The Viale Angelico is wide and tree-lined, with cafes, bars and restaurants on both sides. Dodging pedestrians and pushchairs, we made good time, enough time, I judged, to allow me a fast but much-needed comfort break in one of the eateries.

With The Keeper's 'you'll have to be quick' ringing in my ears, we stopped at a bar and looked in. It was perfect, it had no other customers and a barman with nothing to do. A guaranteed fast service and quick get away. We went in and ordered, and I headed straight for the facilities.

I opened the door off the bar and hit a Goth's paradise. Black walls, black ceiling, black tiles on the floor and just enough subtle lighting to make your way along a corridor, down some steps to a basement and into the ladies. You know you have reached a certain age when the ability to see takes precedence over ambience. If I was not so keen on my mission, this haunted house might have quite put me off.

I was happily engaged under the subtle lighting when suddenly, all the subtlety died, the lights had gone off. *No problem* I thought, *the fitting must be on a timer.* I fumbled around, found the switch and pressed. Hey presto, nothing happened. I could not see a thing.

Stumbling across the bathroom, I found the basin, the soap and the water. Leaving the hand drier for another day, I inched myself along and found the door. Tapping all the walls around the doorframe, I found another switch, hoorah. No, dismay. I was still in darkness. I made it out to the hallway. Walking like a zombie on sedatives, I edged along the wall, shuffling my feet in search of the first step. Finding it, I gingerly took each step until I was on the top and heard voices. It was like coming up for air from a dive. I gingerly made my way along the corridor, found the door, opened it to the daylight in the bar and a clock-watching Keeper.

"What kept you?" asked The Keeper, oblivious to my black hole experience but mindful of the time.

"There wasn't any light, and you had my phone," I uttered feebly whilst applying my backpack to my person.

The Keeper looked confused, but deciding that further questions would just consume time, he turned to the barman instead and asked, "Can we pay?"

"No," came the reply, "there has been a power cut; the till will not open, can you wait?"

We looked at each other, no we could not wait, we had one of the dearest meetings of our lives coming up; we had our family to see. Rifling through our pockets, we assembled the appropriate change, paid and sped off.

Hitting the Via di Porta Angelica, we almost ran to St Peter's Square. Reaching the giant colonnades that embrace the vast elliptical space, we could not help but stop and gasp at their immensity. Then, searching through them, across the throngs of wandering and queuing tourists, we saw what we were looking for.

Banners were flying; arms were waving; a grandchild was being jiggled; and huge, huge smiles were on the faces of our family. In St Peter's Square, under the eyes of the great Basilica and in front of the queuing tourists (many of whom clapped), we hugged each other.

We had made it; we were here; we had walked all the way from our Home to Rome. In the hubbub of the family gathering, I caught The Keeper's eye, and we exchanged smiles. Smiles that silently said, *after all the planning, the long days, the heat, the exhaustion and personal loss, we had made it to the Vatican, and we had done it together*".

Then I looked at my watch. It was 12:06. We had been 6 tiny minutes late.

CONGRATULATIONS

It was slightly tedious that those minutes had been consumed in the black hole of a bathroom, with my knickers around my knees, but I was not complaining.

Anway, did it matter? Who was going to notice or really care? Then I saw The Keeper look at his own watch. I waited for the reaction.

A shrug of the shoulders and a quick grin told me the answer.

GETTING
CERTIFIED
MAP

Every night of our journey, The Keeper and I had collected a stamp in each of our Pilgrim Passports showing where we had stayed. To be able to receive a final stamp and Testimonium from St Peter's Basilica, applicants must prove they have walked at least 140km to Rome. We felt more than qualified, so off we went.

Security, unsurprisingly, was very tight. The nice guard, doing his best to look assertive whilst dressed in the flamboyant red, yellow and blue striped knickerbocker livery of the Vatican City, searched our backpacks and told us where to go.

"You must go to the office. From there, you go straight and take the door under the arch, turn left, go down the hallway, up the stairs, through another door, take a right, and you are there."

As instructed, we went to the office, where they scanned us and our bags and swapped our British passports for visitors' badges. They gave us, again, strict instructions as to where to go.

"You must go straight, then go under the arch and take a door on the left, turn left again, and take the hallway, follow the stairs to another door, turn right."

Off we went. We were just crossing the courtyard, heading for the first instruction, the door under the arch, when we were accosted politely by another pair of knickerbockers. "Do you know where you are going?" the custodian of the knickers asked politely. We nodded, hoping we looked like we did, which we obviously did not as, yet again, we were given a set of exacting instructions.

With the directions now swirling around in our short-term memories we reached a door under the arch and went through. We turned left and went down the hallway as far as some stairs. So far so good. We went up the stairs, found another door and went through. All seemed to be going to plan. We turned right and found ourselves in a long hallway with numerous polished oak doors. All the doors were closed and none of them had signs or numbers; they were just doors. We looked at each other. All was no longer going so well, which door do we take now?

“How about the first door on our right?” suggested The Keeper. We gingerly knocked, but there was no response. We turned the handle and slowly opened the door. Inside was a long, thin room with a curved ceiling. Lining the walls from floor to ceiling were beautiful wooden cabinets and at the point where the cabinets ended and the ceiling arched, were gilt-framed oil portraits of papal and military personnel. There was not, however, an official offering the pilgrimage stamp, so we closed the door.

“Now what do we do?” I whispered.

“We will have to keep trying other doors,” whispered The Keeper.

“Why are we whispering?” I asked.

“I don’t know,” replied The Keeper, still whispering.

We moved on to the next door and knocked again. No one answered. We turned the handle and again, slowly opened the door. Inside were rails and rails of vestments, all neatly pressed and hanging in readiness to be donned. There was not, however, the official we searched for, so we quietly closed the door.

We tried again, one more door along. We knocked and there was no response. We turned the handle and there was still no response, so we slowly opened the door.

And there was a little old nun, busily eating her breakfast.

I am not sure who was more surprised, her or us. I apologised profusely and before she got alarmed and rang for help from the multicoloured knickers, I went into action.

Turning the mute Keeper around as fast as I could, I pointed to his backpack. The nun looked stunned, obviously not quite sure why, if she had been faced with the front of an unwanted visitor, she now needed to see his back. Oh dear. I showed her my visitors’ badge, still no acknowledgement, just a pair of wizened eyes looking questioningly at us from deep within her coif and veil. I opened my pilgrimage passport and held it towards her. Slowly, she looked at it, then at us, her eyes beginning to understand the situation and appreciate the stupidity of those before her.

With a reluctant glance at her breakfast and only half a smile at us, she beckoned us to follow her. To this day, I cannot remember the correct door which she took us to. I do not know whether it was to the left, to the right or opposite; I only know that with a slight nod of relief at not having to deal with us further, the nun left us outside another set of polished oak doors.

We knocked, but as with the other doors, there was no response. By now, we were caught between exasperation and a good dose of the giggles. We slowly opened the door and looked in. The room was immense, more than triple heighted, octagonal in shape and topped with a domed ceiling. Huge marbled grey walls, ornate plasterwork and mouldings, grand pillars and columns all stood before us.

With our heads poked around the door, our eyes searched through the embellishments of the room, trying to find anything that was relevant to us. There were no signs, but against a far wall, we could see a polished wooden desk and a man in uniform (not the knicker livery this time but a more sedate blue shirt and black tie) behind it. The uniformed gentleman was the only person in the room, and he was looking straight at us. At last, we had found our man, we hoped.

Standing before the official at his desk we proffered our pilgrim passports, which he looked at with all the enthusiasm of a turkey at Christmas. Taking hold of a rather disappointingly small and modern stamp he marked our pilgrim passports and issued us each with a Testimonium and a nod. I could not help myself, the victory of finding this chap and receiving the last stamp was too much. Smiling from ear to ear, I did my signature bottom wiggle manoeuvre. The Keeper, resigned to such displays, raised his eyebrows with the unspoken question of *what, here?* He obviously did not realise it was an involuntary reaction. Stamp Man bent his head to his desk (but I did notice a twitch of amusement flick across his face).

That was it, the last and final part of our Home to Rome adventure completed. That is, if we could find our way out...

The Keeper's Data:

Number of footsteps taken between us: 5.3 million

Number of miles walked from our home to the Vatican: 1,450

Number of types of food scavenged en route: 11 (nature's bounty = fig, peach, apple, pear, plum, kiwi, blackberry, hazelnut, walnut, tomato, grape)

Number of friends who joined us at some point en route: 37

Number of friends lost as a consequence: 0 (hopefully)

Number of blisters lanced: 6 (not ours, thankfully)

Number of different beds slept in: 75

Number of eggs cooked in hotel kettles: 18

Number of wayside figs plucked: 67

Number of boots worn out: 6

Number of days the same shirt was worn: 75 out of 75

When she is not out walking Mountain Goat can be reached on
mountaingoat.walks@gmail.com

Matador